BEDFORD BOOKS IN AMERICAN HISTORY

Narrative of the Life of Frederick Douglass, An American Slave, Written by Himself

BEDFORD BOOKS IN AMERICAN HISTORY
Ernest R. May, Advisory Editor

The Autobiography of Benjamin Franklin
Edited with an introduction by Louis P. Masur, *City University of New York*

Narrative of the Life of Frederick Douglass, An American Slave, Written by Himself
Edited with an introduction by David W. Blight, *Amherst College*

Plunkitt of Tammany Hall by William L. Riordon
Edited with an introduction by Terrence J. McDonald, *The University of Michigan*

American Cold War Strategy: Interpreting NSC 68
Edited with an introduction by Ernest R. May, *Harvard University*

BEDFORD BOOKS IN AMERICAN HISTORY

Narrative of the Life of Frederick Douglass, An American Slave, Written by Himself

Edited with an introduction by

David W. Blight

Amherst College

BEDFORD BOOKS *of* ST. MARTIN'S PRESS

Boston • New York

For Bedford Books

Publisher: Charles H. Christensen
Associate Publisher/General Manager: Joan E. Feinberg
History Editor: Sabra Scribner
Associate History Editor: Louise D. Townsend
Managing Editor: Elizabeth M. Schaaf
Copyeditor: Susan M. S. Brown
Text Design: Claire Seng-Niemoeller
Cover Design: Richard Emery Design
Cover Art: Detail from a photograph of Frederick Douglass, 1818–1895; Unidentified photographer; Ambrotype, 1856; The National Portrait Gallery, Smithsonian Institution; Gift of an anonymous donor.

Library of Congress Cataloging-in-Publication Data
Douglass, Frederick, 1817?–1895.
Narrative of the life of Frederick Douglass, an American slave, written by himself.
Edited with an introduction by David W. Blight.
    p. cm. (Bedford books in American history)
Includes bibliographical references and index.
ISBN 0–312–09667–4 (cloth).   ISBN 0–312–07531–6 (pbk).
    1. Douglass, Frederick, 1817?–1895.   2. Afro-Americans—Biography.   3. Abolitionists—United States—Biography.   I. Blight, David W.   II. Title.   III. Series.
E449.D749   1993   973.8'.092—dc20   [B]

Library of Congress Catalog Card Number: 92–61004

Manufactured in the United States of America.

7   6   5   4   3

f   e   d   c   b   a

For information, write: St. Martin's Press, Inc., 175 Fifth Avenue, New York, NY 10010
Editorial Offices: Bedford Books *of* St. Martin's Press, 29 Winchester Street, Boston, MA 02116

ISBN: 0–312–07531–6   (paperback)
ISBN: 0–312–09667–4   (hardcover)

Acknowledgments

Page xii: Courtesy of the National Portrait Gallery, Smithsonian Institution.
Pages 27 and 100: Courtesy of the Prints and Photographs Collection, Moorland Spingarn Research Center, Howard University.
Page 46: Courtesy of the Maryland Historical Society.
Page 146: Courtesy of the Library of Congress.

Foreword

The *Bedford Books in American History* series is designed so that readers can study history as historians do.

A historian's mind is a courtroom. There, documents are tested and compared. Eyewitnesses are quizzed. (The dead lie or make mistakes as often as the living. Their memoirs have to be cross-examined.) The historian's mind also takes expert testimony—from other historians and scholars—and tests for bias or contradiction. At some point, the jury determines the likely facts. The historian then turns judge, deciding how those facts mesh and what should be made of them.

At the heart of each book in the series is an important document or group of documents. These are raw sources, open to being interpreted in many different ways. Each book also includes expert commentary from one or more historians exposing various ways of interpreting the sources. Sifting the evidence and argumentation calls for both critical thinking *and* creative imagination.

Each book in the series focuses on a specific topic or period. Each provides a basis for lively thought and discussion about several aspects of the topic or period. Each provides a basis also for debate more generally about the historian's methods and craft. Each is short enough (and inexpensive enough) to be a reasonable one-week assignment in a college course. Whether as an assignment or just as personal reading, each book in the series provides firsthand experience of the challenge—and fun—of recreating and interpreting the past.

Ernest R. May

Preface

Narrative of the Life of Frederick Douglass, An American Slave is a great story about the meaning of slavery and freedom in antebellum America. The most artistically crafted and widely read of all the American slave narratives, Douglass's first of three autobiographies is at once a work of imaginative literature, abolitionist argument, and historical analysis. This edition is intended especially for use by historians and in history courses. Douglass's *Narrative* is a classic illustration of the will to power as the will to write, of physical and psychological liberation through language. It must therefore be treated as a literary text, as indeed it has been by numerous literary critics and by the editors of most previous editions. But this work must also be treated in its historical contexts. Douglass's *Narrative* provides a remarkable window into the world of oppression, cunning, and survival in which slaves lived, as well as the religious and ideological world of abolitionism from which the book emerged in the 1840s. The introductory essay is intended to help readers understand those worlds in which Douglass came of age as a man thinking; it offers a guide for crossing the borders between the modern reader's imagination and the real experience of slavery in an America that was dividing and heading toward civil war.

This edition, moreover, provides the first extensive annotation of Douglass's tale of bondage, escape, and self-made public career. The ending of the *Narrative*—the fugitive slave's emergence as a Garrisonian abolitionist orator and fierce critic of American religious hypocrisy—is much less a climax in Douglass's life than it may appear. It represents only one stage in his dramatic biography, and I have therefore included an extensive chronology at the back of the book.

A recurring message in this work is that to Douglass slavery meant bondage of the mind as much as of the body. After a period of especially harsh treatment under a brutal overseer to whom he was hired out, Douglass described himself as "broken in body, soul, and spirit. My natural elasticity was crushed, my intellect languished, the disposition to read departed, the cheerful spark that lingered about my eye died; the dark night of slavery closed in upon me; and behold a man transformed into a brute!" This book was Douglass's quest to authenticate himself, to claim a free identity, and to issue his own unique indictment of slavery. It was also his effort to work through an anguished past representative of many African American slaves, to "pour out," as he said, "his soul's complaint." Thus, from reading Douglass's *Narrative,* we can behold much more than the human made chattel. Behold how the slave became a man, how the field hand became a man with a mind, and how the fugitive slave became an abolitionist lecturer and the author of one of the greatest works of antislavery literature in the nineteenth century. But behold as well a deeply imagined story about the universal human quest for real, self-conscious freedom.

ACKNOWLEDGMENTS

I have accumulated many intellectual and professional debts in editing this volume and writing the introductory essay. The series editor, Ernest May, has been kind and encouraging; his reading of a draft of the introduction was extremely helpful. I have enjoyed working with the splendid staff at Bedford Books: Chuck Christensen, Joan Feinberg, Louise Townsend, Elizabeth Schaaf, Susan Brown, and especially the history editor, Sabra Scribner. I owe much to the scholarly influence, personal support, and critical readings of William McFeely, David Brion Davis, and Waldo Martin. I am also grateful for the careful editing and suggestions of Joanne Fraser, John Inscoe, and Eliza McFeely. Many colleagues have helped me to better understand Douglass and his *Narrative* during the preparation of this volume. Among them are Robert Gooding-Williams, David Wills, Robert O'Meally, Margaret Washington, Werner Sollors, Berndt Ostendorf, Alessandro Portelli, and Klaus Ensslen. I could not have prepared the annotations without the help of Amherst College librarians Margaret Groesbeck, Floyd Merritt, and Janice Denton. James Alec Dunn was an excellent research assistant. The work of William Andrews and Henry Louis Gates, Jr., on the slave narratives has been indispensable. And, as always, I am grateful to Karin Beckett for sharing many years and many critical discussions with me and with Frederick Douglass.

David W. Blight

Contents

Frederick Douglass, probably his first photograph, taken in his twenties

Introduction:
"A Psalm of Freedom"

Memory was given to man for some wise purpose. The past is ... the mirror in which we may discern the dim outlines of the future and by which we may make them more symmetrical. —Frederick Douglass, 1884

Therefore I will not refrain my mouth; I will speak in the anguish of my spirit; I will complain in the bitterness of my soul. —Job 7:11

Frederick Douglass was the most important African American leader and intellectual of the nineteenth century. He lived twenty years as a slave and nearly nine years as a fugitive slave; from the 1840s to his death in 1895, he attained international fame as an abolitionist, reformer, editor, orator, and the author of three autobiographies, which are classics of the slave narrative tradition. As a man of affairs, he began his abolitionist career two decades before America would divide and fight a tragic civil war over slavery. He lived to see black emancipation, to work actively for women's suffrage long before it was achieved, to realize the civil rights triumphs and tragedies of Reconstruction, and to witness America's economic and international expansion in the late Gilded Age. He lived until the eve of the Age of Jim Crow (racial segregation), when America seemed in retreat from the very victories in race relations that he had helped to win.

Although Douglass lived long and witnessed many great events, perhaps his most important contribution to American history was the repeated telling of his personal story. Above all else, this book, *Narrative of the Life of Frederick Douglass,* is a great story told, like most other great stories, out of the will to be known and the will to write. This tale of a young African American's journey into and out of slavery provides a remarkable window on America's most compelling nineteenth-century social and political problem. In this introductory essay, several historical and literary themes will be explored as a guide for student readers. Such a guide may be useful either before or after reading the text. Some may wish to plunge right into Douglass's first chapter, a classic polemic against slavery's hostility to family life. Others may wish to read this introduction first and consider its many suggestions about the content and meaning of the text for American history. Either way, Douglass is, of course, his own uniquely informed, sometimes manipulative guide to his experience.

Douglass saw to the core of the meaning of slavery, both for individuals and for the nation. Likewise, the multiple meanings of freedom—as idea and reality, of mind and body—and of the consequences of its denial were his great themes. In 1855 he offered this timeless explanation of his hatred of slavery and his desire for freedom: "The thought of only being a creature of the *present* and the *past,* troubled me, and I longed to have a *future*—a future with hope in it. To be shut up entirely to the past and present is abhorrent to the human mind; it is to the soul—whose life and happiness is unceasing progress—what the prison is to the body." No genre of literature has offered better descriptions of the meaning of hope, of the liberation of mind, body, and soul—that sense of future Douglass named—than the slave narratives. Douglass probed his past throughout his life, seeking to understand the relentless connection of past and present, telling his story in relation to the turbulent history of his time, and hoping to control or stop time itself. But, like all great autobiographers, he would only discover how memory is both absolutely essential and bewilderingly deceptive as a means to self-understanding.[1]

Douglass was born Frederick Augustus Washington Bailey in the cabin of his grandmother Betsey Bailey along Tuckahoe Creek, in Talbot County, Maryland, in February 1818. His mother, Harriet Bailey, was a slave owned by Aaron Anthony, a former Chesapeake schooner captain and an overseer on a large Eastern Shore plantation. Douglass saw his mother for the last time when he was seven, making him in every practical way an orphan. The actual identity of his father is still unknown, but he was undoubtedly white, as Douglass declares in the *Narrative*. Douglass was, therefore, of mixed racial ancestry, including part American Indian, which came from his grand-mother's family. As readers will readily see, Douglass's twenty years in slavery were marked by stark contrasts between brutality and good fortune, between the life of a favored slave youth in Baltimore and that of a field hand on an Eastern Shore farm, and between the power of literacy and the despair born of its suppression. The Frederick Bailey who became Frederick Doug-lass after his escape had a story well worth telling, and American and British audiences would be eager to read it.

In 1845 Douglass felt compelled by many factors to write his story. His extraordinary life as a slave, the circumstances of his escape, his emergence as a skillful abolitionist lecturer in the early 1840s, and suspicions as well as bigoted denials that so talented a voice could ever have been a chattel slave combined with the sheer popularity of slave narratives to prompt him to tell his tale. On September 3, 1838, at the age of twenty, Douglass, disguised as a sailor and having obtained the papers of a free seaman, escaped from slavery on the eastern shore of the Chesapeake in Maryland.[2] Within a week he was joined by his fiancée, Anna Murray, a free black woman from Baltimore. David Ruggles, the black abolitionist leader of the New York Vigilance Committee (one of a network of urban organizations by which the Underground Railroad operated), helped provide Frederick and Anna safe haven, which was no simple matter for fugitive slaves in the 1830s. On September 15 they were married by Rev. James W. C. Pennington, himself an escaped slave from Maryland's Eastern Shore. The Douglasses quickly moved from New York City to New Bedford, Massachusetts, a thriving port town with a significant free black population and where it was believed Douglass could ply his trade as a ship's caulker.[3] It was there that Douglass and the growing band of Massachusetts abolitionists discovered each other during the next three years.

In its content and its strategies, therefore, Douglass's *Narrative* belonged to the world of abolitionism and to the national political crisis over slavery from which it sprang. Douglass's autobiographies are our principal sources for major aspects of his life, especially his early years. But they are perhaps as revelatory of the history of the times through which he lived as they are of his personality and his psychology. Close readings of the *Narrative* uncover not only Douglass's rhetorical strategies, which are many and complicated, but also a good deal about the moral and economic nature of slavery, the master-slave relationship, the psychology of slaveholders, the aims and arguments of abolitionists, and the impending political crisis between North and South that would lead to the Civil War.

Douglass's personal story, like American history itself, is both inspiring and terrible. Few writers have better combined experience with the music of words to make us see the deepest contradictions of American history, the tragedy and necessity of conflict between slavery and freedom in a republic. Douglass exposes the bitterness and absurdity of racism at the same time that he imagines the fullest possibilities of the natural rights tradition, the idea that people are born with equal rights in the eyes of God and that those rights can be protected under human law. Few have written more effectively about the endurance of the human spirit under oppression. And in American letters, we have no better illustration of liberation through the power of language than in Douglass's *Narrative*. With his pen, Douglass was very much a self-conscious artist, and with his voice and his activism, he was a self-conscious prophet.

Readers of the *Narrative* quickly come to realize that language, written and oratorical, had been a fascination and a weapon for Douglass during his years as a slave. When he first spoke before a meeting of New Bedford blacks against African colonization in March 1839, and when he delivered his first public speeches before a gathering of the Massachusetts Anti-Slavery Society on Nantucket Island in August 1841, he was not merely appearing as the spontaneous abolitionist miracle he was often portrayed—and portrayed himself—to be. No doubt the first effort at "speaking to white people" at the Nantucket meeting was a "severe cross," as he describes the experience in the *Narrative*.[4] But Douglass was no stranger to oratory, or to the moral arguments, sentimentalism, and evangelical zeal that characterized the antislavery movement during that era. By 1841 he had been reading abolitionist speeches, editorials, and poetry in William Lloyd Garrison's newspaper, *The Liberator,* for at least two years. And as the *Narrative* tells us in a variety of ways, Douglass had been a practicing abolitionist of a kind—out of self-interest and for his fellow bondsmen—even while he was a slave. He had read the Bible extensively, and he had discovered and modeled his ideas and style on a remarkable 1797 book, *The Columbian Orator,* by Caleb Bingham, a selection from which is reproduced in this volume.

From the earliest period of his public career, Douglass knew that whether in the slave South or in the free North to which he had liberated himself, literacy was power. The nineteenth-century Western world owed much of its values and mores to the eighteenth-century Enlightenment's faith in human reason and its assertion of individual rights. To be judged truly human and a citizen with social and political recognition, therefore, a person had to achieve literacy. For better or worse, civilization itself was equated with cultures that could *write* their history. Hence, writes Henry Louis Gates, Jr., Douglass became an American "Representative Man because he was Rhetorical Man, black master of the verbal arts. Douglass is our clearest example of the will to power as the will to write. The act of writing for the slave constituted the act of creating a public, historical self."[5]

The Douglass who spoke at Nantucket was quickly hired by Garrison and the Massachusetts Anti-Slavery Society to be a traveling lecturer, first around New England and eventually across the North. Thus the fugitive slave found his voice and his calling. From 1841 to 1845, on almost countless platforms, Douglass began to tell the "free story" that he would soon publish to great acclaim in the *Narrative*.[6]

In many ways Douglass's *Narrative* is a careful, artistic summing up of the many speeches he had delivered in the three years he spent on the abolitionist lecture circuit before he sat down in 1844 to create his own character and to try to make the world stop seeing him as a mere curiosity. To tell his story of suffering and liberation from slavery on platforms was one thing; to publish it for a reading public eager for the tales of escaped slaves was quite another. On the lecture platform it might appear that he only told stories. But in the *Narrative* he sought authentication. He wanted the world to know that fugitive slaves had histories. His book would make witness to the fact, contrary to popular attitudes, that blacks too were people, whose struggles and aspirations mattered in human society.

Douglass's oratorical brilliance, the "curiosity" of his audiences, and the relationship of the *Narrative* to the style and content of his early speeches are attested to by two addresses reprinted in this volume. The first, delivered in Concord, New Hampshire, February 11, 1844, and recorded by Nathaniel P. Rogers, offers a striking picture not only of Douglass "narrating his early life" but also of an angry young man who insists that Americans imagine slavery as a scene of horror. Rogers's description of the rhetorical pivot in the speech is stunning: Douglass finished narrating the story and "gradually let out the outraged humanity that was laboring in him, in indignant and terrible speech. It was not what you could describe as oratory or eloquence. It was sterner—darker—deeper than these. It was the volcanic outbreak of human nature long pent up in slavery and at last bursting its imprisonment." Undoubtedly, some of those prison metaphors soon to appear in the *Narrative* emerged in the speech Rogers heard. Rogers was an abolitionist newspaper editor and adept in his own way at antislavery propaganda, but he seems to have been convinced that he had just listened to a latter-day prophet whose "terrible voice" would one day "ring through the pine glades of the South, in the day of her visitation." He was surely right in his observation that he had watched "an insurgent slave taking hold on the right of speech."[7] Shortly after this speech, Douglass was hard at work writing the *Narrative*. The second speech reprinted here was delivered in New York City on May 6, 1845, only a little over a week after Douglass finished writing the *Narra-*

tive and just three weeks before it was published. It is believed to be the first time he divulged numerous specific facts about his slave background beyond the general contours of the story which he had told many times. Both speeches provide a historical and rhetorical context in which to read the *Narrative*.

Although antislavery sentiment emerged in a variety of ways during the age of the American Revolution, the formative decades of organized abolitionism were the 1820s and 1830s, the period in which Frederick Bailey grew up a slave in Maryland. In the *Narrative,* following the moving passages about his achievement of literacy and the discovery of the human rights impulses in *The Columbian Orator,* Douglass describes his gradual realization of the antebellum meaning of the words *abolition* and *abolitionist:* He "always drew near" when those words were spoken, "expecting to hear something of importance to myself and fellow-slaves. The light broke in upon me by degrees." With the life-giving power of literacy also came, as Douglass so honestly puts it, an "unutterable anguish." "It opened my eyes to the horrible pit, but to no ladder upon which to get out." Literacy afforded the young Douglass a whole world of thought, stirring dreams of freedom thwarted at every visible turn of his daily life. The truly thoughtful slave, as Douglass's master had predicted, was a desperately discontented one. Such slaves possessed a language by which to imagine freedom, but this awareness only made their condition more wretched. "It was this everlasting thinking of my condition that tormented me," writes Douglass. But "every little while," he remembers taking heart, because, as he says, "I could hear something about the abolitionists."[8]

What he heard, and read in Baltimore newspapers, were stories of organized groups who sent petitions to the U.S. government demanding the abolition of slavery in the District of Columbia as well as the interstate slave trade. He learned of activists who published their own antislavery newspapers and crusaded to change the condition in which he lived. He realized that many of those abolitionists considered slaveholding a mortal sin. Above all else perhaps, he gained the simple awareness that in the northern states slavery either did not exist or was rapidly dying out. Some of the reformers he read about would turn out to be racist and patronizing, but some of them would provide the community, friendship, and mentorship in which Douglass found his life's work. As he sat on a crate during break time as a caulker in the dockyards of Baltimore, or lamented away afternoons on William Freeland's farm on the Eastern Shore, he realized in half-formed ways, as he had learned from *The Columbian Orator* and the Bible in metaphorical ways, that up there in the free North there was an "argument" about slavery.[9]

Under the influence of evangelical religion, a growing realization of southern commitment to slavery, and especially the British antislavery movement, American abolitionists found their ideological roots in the 1820s. The campaign to end slavery in the British Empire profoundly shook the increasingly active defenders of slavery in the American South and helped to cause a steady radicalization of antislavery tactics in the North. After 1831, when William Lloyd Garrison founded *The Liberator* in Boston, as abolitionist societies sprang up across the North, and as a growing number of fugitive slaves and other free blacks entered the movement on their own behalf, American abolitionism became an organized crusade. By 1838, the year Douglass escaped from slavery, the movement had flooded Congress with petitions, experienced intense and deadly antiabolition violence, awakened a defiant South, and caused many conversions in the reformist North. It had also fomented the beginnings of antislavery political parties and, like most great reform movements, fallen into bitter factional dispute. Douglass was deeply inspired by Garrison himself, and by his newspaper. When he fell in with the Garrisonians in 1841, they represented the largest and most radical wing of the antislavery movement.

Garrison and many of his loyal followers were fierce radicals; they devoted their lives to ridding America of slavery and worked vigorously to eliminate discrimination against blacks and women in northern society. They roamed the frontiers of reform ideology in antebellum America. By the late 1830s, Garrison himself had taken some positions that increasing numbers of abolitionists found untenable and impractical. He denounced churches, the U.S. Constitution, political parties, and voting itself as institutional or personal complicity with the evil of slaveholding. "No Union With the Slaveholders," part of the masthead of *The Liberator,* became the slogan of a Garrisonian doctrine of "disunion," which urged northern abolitionists to sever all political and religious ties to the South. Such a plan would, through a strange logic, isolate slaveholders and their accomplices under the blinding light of moral condemnation and lead to emancipation through peaceful, ethical renewal. This was the doctrine of "moral suasion" taken to its fullest extent: The hearts and minds of the American people were first to be persuaded of the evil of slavery, then the laws and political structure would change.

After returning from his first trip to England in 1847, and having experienced a growing sense of organizational and intellectual independence, Douglass broke with his Garrisonian comrades in a protracted and bitter dispute. This split with his first abolitionist mentor had both ideological and personal causes. In the late 1840s and early 1850s, especially after his move to Rochester, New York, and the founding of his own newspaper, the *North Star,* Douglass became a more open, though no less committed, pragmatist about antislavery tactics. Under new influences, especially the New York abolitionist and philanthropist Gerrit Smith, Douglass came to believe that the Constitution could be used to exert federal power against slavery, especially its expansion into the West. He also embraced the use of political parties, and eventually even certain instances of violence, as a means of destroying slavery (through the political system or outside of it). Moreover, during and after his two-and-a-half-year tour of the British Isles, and because of his brilliant oratory, the impact of the *Narrative,* and the force of his personality, Douglass became an international star of the abolition movement. Simply put, he became a visible, independent, and less doctrinaire rival to the Garrisonians' leadership of the American antislavery movement.[10]

Readers of the 1845 *Narrative,* however, will find many influences of Garrisonian doctrines, especially the attacks on religious hypocrisy and the remarkable moment in Chapter 2 when Douglass compares trusted slaves who pleased overseers with the "slaves of the political parties."[11] Indeed, like most slave narratives, the book is as much an abolitionist polemic as it is a revealing autobiography. What sets Douglass's work apart in the genre, though, is that he interrogated the moral conscience of his readers, at the same time that he transplanted them into his story, as few other fugitive slave writers did.

Douglass's writing is not cautious; he pays little regard to the tender sensibilities of his readers, and he is willing to manipulate their deepest fears and passions. Garrison's preface, itself a masterly piece of antislavery propaganda, attests to these qualities in Douglass's language: The mentor celebrates the substance and style of the "terrible chastisements," the "shocking outrages," and the continual access Douglass allows to "how he thought, reasoned, felt, under the lash of the driver, with the chains upon his limbs!" As William S. McFeely and William L. Andrews have suggested, Douglass's *Narrative* shares kinship with Walt Whitman's *Leaves of Grass,* published a decade later; it too is a "Song of Myself." Even more, it may have influenced another great work of self-emancipation, Henry David Thoreau's *Walden.*[12] But mostly, Douglass's *Narrative* is a song of abolitionism, an argument with America's conscience, an appeal by the risen slave testifying to his own sufferings and making witness to the crimes of a guilty land.

As the literary critic Robert G. O'Meally has argued, Douglass's *Narrative* was, "in its way, a holy book . . . a text meant, of course, to be read, but . . . also a text meant to be mightily preached." The book is imbued with biblical references, imagery, and metaphors, and it owes much to the black sermonic tradition from which Douglass had learned a great deal about the use of language and its powers. His exhortative tones and rhythms not only were modeled on the Old Testament prophets Douglass read but were undoubtedly the ones he had practiced among his band of brothers at the Sabbath school on Freeland's farm, as he and his charges learned to plot their own deliverance as well as to keep faith in one another and in God. Indeed, from Garrison's preface to Douglass's appendix about the perils of religious hypocrisy in slaveholding America, the work is framed and conceived as, in O'Meally's apt description,

> a warning of the terror of God's fury. It is also an account of the black Moses' flight from "slavery to freedom." It is an invitation to join "the church" of abolition, a church that offers freedom not only to the slave and the sympathetic white Northerner but also to the most murderous and bloodthirsty Southern dealers in human flesh. Sinners, Douglass seems to chant, black sermon–style, you are in the hands of an angry God![13]

Douglass's burning contempt for "pious slaveholders" was not merely abolitionist propaganda, as it is too often portrayed. It was the fuel, the bitterly ironic energy of a spiritual autobiography.

Douglass's *Narrative,* like much of his oratory, also fits squarely into one of America's oldest literary traditions: the jeremiad. Named for the book of Jeremiah, and appropriated in America since the seventeenth-century Puritan sermons that chastised Christians for their declining faith, the jeremiad became a kind of political sermon and a literary form—functioning not only as a lamentation about waning zeal but also as a national ritual of both self-condemnation and optimistic assertions of the American mythology of mission. As the historian Wilson J. Moses has contended, jeremiads took on special urgency in the language of black abolitionists; they became the "constant warnings" issued to white audiences "concerning the judgment that was to come for the sin of slavery." On hundreds of platforms Douglass had lent his voice to this ritual like no other black abolitionist. And in writing the *Narrative,* William L. Andrews has suggested, Douglass announced not only his literary calling but also "his ultimate self-appointment as America's black Jeremiah."[14]

Douglass's *Narrative* appealed to readers in his own time for many reasons. Midnineteenth-century American readers were very familiar with jeremiads that reminded them of America's divinely appointed mission and of such betrayals of that mission as slavery. They might have been both troubled by and attracted to narratives about true and false Americanism. They were especially drawn to escape from captivity narratives, to tales of self-made men and self-liberation. And, perhaps most of all, readers were at home with spiritual autobiographies—ritualistic testimonies about the trial of the soul as well as the body, journeys from mental and spiritual darkness through severe tests to the light of regeneration.[15]

In one of the most memorable passages of the *Narrative,* Douglass remembers the terrible year he lived as a sixteen-year-old under the wrath of the slave breaker Edward Covey: It was his "dark night of slavery," a time when he often felt "transformed into a brute," and when he spent whole days "mourning over my wretched condition." But all of this frames a story of resurrection and an unforgettable image of freedom. The Covey farm was only a short distance from Chesapeake Bay, and on its banks Douglass places himself, changing voice to the nearly suicidal sixteen-year-old slave, pouring out his "soul's complaint" in a psalmlike prayer for deliverance. The white-sailed vessels on the bay are "shrouded ghosts" that torment him one moment and become the dreamlike objects of his lonely prayer the next: "You are loosed from your moorings, and are free; I am fast in my chains, and am a slave! You move merrily before the gentle gale, and I sadly before the bloody whip! You are freedom's swift-winged angels, that fly round the world; I am confined in bands of iron!" Here Douglass reveals a mind and soul made captive, but, through moral imagination and belief in "a better day coming," he keeps faith and wills his own freedom.[16]

In this famous passage Douglass reaches an early height in his craft as a writer and demonstrates the influence of the Negro spirituals and of the Psalms on his temperament. Appealing for deliverance from enemies and testifying to tattered but refurbished faith, Douglass writes what might best be called his own psalm, or a prose poem, about the meaning of freedom. In the decade before the Civil War, readers of the *Narrative* could sit with Douglass in the dark night of his soul along their own Chesapeakes and sense the deepest of human yearnings in their own souls. Today's readers can do so as well.

Well into the twentieth century, slave narratives were not considered proper historical sources for the study of slavery. They were deemed inauthentic and biased by Ulrich B. Phillips, the first major historian of slavery to make extensive use of plantation records. Phillips did not acknowledge that ex-slaves left any genuine testimony on what plantation slavery was really like. His *American Negro Slavery* (1918), the most authoritative work on the subject as late as the 1950s, pictured slavery as a patriarchal, benign institution in which masters and slaves acted out largely natural roles of fatherlike masters and chattel laborers. In Phillips's work, the slaves were the beneficiaries of a system that maintained white supremacy and an agricultural order. This "plantation legend"—an Old South living a kind of golden age in which the masters provided and the slaves labored in relative contentment—died hard in American historiography and still survives in popular culture. The most enduring examples of that survival come from motion pictures and popular fiction, especially the eternal, worldwide fascination with *Gone With the Wind*.[17]

But the revolution of interest in black history, which coincided with the modern civil rights movement in the 1950s and 1960s, brought a renewed attention to and use of the slave narratives.[18] The first modern edition of Douglass's *Narrative* was published in 1960, and many other first-person accounts of bondage were brought back into print through the next decade and a half. Historians began to make careful use of the slave narratives as sources of historical information and, perhaps more important, as guides to the slaves' perspective on their own felt experience. With the works of John Blassingame, Eugene Genovese, Herbert Gutman, Lawrence Levine, and several others in the 1970s, the slave narratives emerged from obscurity and became a major tool by which historians were able to open the world the slaves made—their folk life, religious expression, modes of resistance and psychological survival.[19]

In this major shift in methodology, the use of previously suspect sources, and the rich analysis that flowed from it, we can see a prime example of how perceptions of historical truth can markedly change. Single documents and texts can be interpreted in different ways and from different perspectives. Indeed, historians can be directly influenced by the events and values in their own era; at the same time they must strictly adhere to evidence in order to seek the truth as they can best determine it. What actually happened in the past does not really change, of course. But the questions we choose to ask of the past change, and thereby new interpretations emerge. This is what is really meant by learning something new from or about the past. The questions change and thus yield new understandings. This is why, as historians often say, each generation must write its own history. From the 1960s, the old, neglected slave narratives, Douglass's in particular, became sources that had new uses and meanings.

What, indeed, was it like to be a slave? What were the slaves' daily feelings, yearnings, crises, and hardships? The best of the slave narratives offer complex answers to these questions. In spite of the propagandistic nature of a work like Douglass's *Narrative,* its principal historical value may be the access it allows us to the psychological world of a slave who had determined to be free. Although it is full of the language of the self-made hero ascending to his destiny and manipulates readers with the purple prose of sentimentalism, a close reading of Douglass's *Narrative* reveals much about the slave's inner torments. His descriptions of the loving bonds he shared with his pupils at the Sabbath school on Freeland's farm and his romantic but altogether believable images of the fears he and his fellows faced in plotting their escape serve as examples of the self-conscious artist struggling to recapture real experience. Douglass looks back to his Sabbath school "with an amount of pleasure not to be expressed. They were great days to my soul." But the love he still feels for his band of brothers mixes with the memory of the "odds" and "obstacles" they faced in contemplating flight. "The thought was truly a horrible one," remembers Douglass, and he converts the memory into a mixture of metaphors and terrible opposites:

> At every gate through which we were to pass, we saw a watchman—at every ferry a guard—on every bridge a sentinel—and in every wood a patrol. We were hemmed in upon every side. Here were the difficulties, real or imagined—the good to be sought, and the evil to be shunned. On the one hand, there stood slavery, a stern reality, glaring frightfully upon us,—its robes already crimsoned with the blood of millions, and even now feasting itself greedily upon our own flesh. On the other hand, away back in the dim distance, under the flickering light of the north star, behind some craggy hill or snow-covered mountain, stood a doubtful freedom— half frozen—beckoning us to come and share its hospitality.[20]

Thus could knowledge about the difference between slavery and freedom manifest in the ex-slave's imagination and, in turn, in that of his readers. Slavery, like all historical experience, must be imagined before it can be understood.

Alternating between parody and condemnation, one of the most persistent themes in Douglass's *Narrative* is his portrait of slaveholders. A striking feature of the book is the sheer range of slaveholders Douglass presents. Examples of unmitigated evil and depravity include Covey, Andrew Anthony (Master Andrew), and Orson (called Austin) Gore. Thomas Auld, both cruel and incompetent, is distinguished for his "meanness" but disrespected for his haplessness. At the other end of the human scale, though, we meet William Freeland, a master Douglass seems to have respected because he was educated, sought no religious sanction for slavery, and ran an economically efficient plantation where work expectations and treatment seemed in rational relationship. And, finally, there is Sophia Auld, Douglass's "kind and tender-hearted" mistress in Baltimore who first taught him to read. She becomes Douglass's principal example that slaveholding is learned behavior, and presumably can therefore be unlearned. In a document so full of antislavery propaganda, physical violence, and suffering, it may come as some surprise that Douglass could conclude that, for Sophia, "slavery proved as injurious to her as it did to me."[21] But such is the complex argument of this highly crafted narrative: It is a picture of a world that not only involved brutal dehumanization but also operated by the cunning and negotiation of human relationships.

This was, in part, the point of Douglass's famous 1848 public letter to Thomas Auld, reprinted in this volume. The letter, written after Douglass's freedom had been purchased for him by his British antislavery friends, is a highly polemical, at times factually inaccurate (see headnote with letter), attack on Auld as a prototypically evil slaveholder. The highly personal, even sensational, charges Douglass makes against Auld do not mask his honest admission at the end of the letter. In words so many slaves must have dreamed they could one day say as freedpeople to their masters, Douglass announces that "I intend to make use of you as a weapon with which to assail the system of slavery . . . and as a means of bringing this guilty nation with yourself to repentance."[22] Again Douglass mingles his personal story, its villains and its self-made hero, with his claims of national birthright.

Although the slave narratives have limitations as sources for the daily, material lives of slaves, as well as for the socioeconomic structure of the antebellum South, Douglass's account is a window into slave work and culture. In Chapter 2 Douglass allows us to observe the huge Wye plantation—the Great House Farm—in operation. We can almost see its bustling "business-like aspect," and hear the "driver's horn" and the profanity of an overseer's voice in the field. In Chapters 3 and 4, slaves are shown to be the essential laborers at the center of southern economic production, but their work is framed and overwhelmed by the larger story of the potentially total power of masters and overseers. The overseer, Austin Gore, appears as a kind of absolute creation of the slave system—a grave, humorless man who performed all his duties, including the murder of insubordinate slaves, with military precision.[23] Douglass strives to describe the most terrible meanings of slavery—its existence outside any law or social control and its capacity to render African American life of no value.

The theme of family separation, a staple of abolitionist argument, emerges in all its potential capriciousness in Chapter 8. Frederick's old master had died, and the ten-year-old was forced to return from Baltimore to the Wye plantation on the Eastern Shore "to be valued with the other property." Douglass's frequent use of animal imagery was never so stark, and his sense of the slaves' anxiety about being sold South is palpable: "Our fate for life was now to be decided. We had no more voice in that decision than the brutes among whom we were ranked." Douglass was luckier than many of his relatives; he was sent back to Baltimore rather than to a much harsher fate on the Eastern Shore or at the hands of the "Georgia traders."[24]

Douglass's *Narrative,* like others in the genre, often reads like a tale of unremitting woe and dehumanization. This was, indeed, one of the aims of the private story converted to public, abolitionist purposes. Reading audiences in the 1840s had to be shocked before they could become a source of sociopolitical action. The five murders Douglass sketches in Chapter 4 and the family separations are tales of lawlessness and rightlessness in republican and Christian America. They point to the deep ironies, as well as a very American quality, of the book: As a Garrisonian at this stage in his career, Douglass could denounce politics and religious hypocrisy at the same time that he wrote with his own heartfelt political and religious motivations.

Douglass's rich use of irony leads us, finally, to an understanding of the complexities of slave resistance. Colonel Lloyd's magnificent garden was exotic and the object of admiration, but it also became for the slaves an education in both the risks and the righteousness of "stealing fruit." The totalitarian capacity of masters to sell their slaves away for profit or spite is balanced with the slaves' control of their own language: The slaveholders' power was blunted by the slaves' "maxim, that a still tongue makes a wise head. They suppress the truth rather than take the consequences of telling it, and in so doing prove themselves a part of the human family."[25] Thus, Douglass argues, the slaves' *humanity* manifests in their cunning accommodation to and subversion of evil authority.

Douglass makes this point most subtly, and anticipates modern historians' treatment of slave culture most directly, in his discussion of slave music. He portrays the slave songs as primarily expressions of sorrow and lament, but he also indicates the inseparability of the sacred and the secular in black folk music, of everyday life mixed with appeals for deliverance in "the most rapturous tone." The scene in which he discusses music is, after all, that of a mass of slaves walking toward the Great House Farm on "allowance-day." The "dense old woods . . . reverberate" with song as groups of selected slaves congregate at Colonel Lloyd's mansion for their periodic allotments of food and clothing. Here, Douglass brilliantly juxtaposes the dehumanizing power structure of slavery with the slaves' own best means of inner relief and self-expression. He even leaves an invitation to modern historians and folk-lorists: "If any one wishes to be impressed with the soul-killing effects of slavery, let him go to Colonel Lloyd's plantation, and, on allowance-day, place himself in the deep pine woods, and there let him, in silence, analyze the sounds that shall pass through the chambers of his soul." Since the 1960s, this is precisely what historians like Lawrence Levine, Sterling Stuckey, Leon Litwack, and others have done with the lyrics and forms of slave music. Scholars have found various ways to gain access to the piney woods, to listen to the slaves' own voices, as they created an inner moral order out of potential chaos and forged what Levine has called an "improvisational communal consciousness."[26] Although intended as confrontational abolitionist literature in its context, Douglass's *Narrative* has been used as a crucial source in the most significant revolution in slavery historiography in our time—the use of folklore and slave autobiographies themselves as sources for understanding how slaves created a culture of resistance amidst oppression.

Slave narratives are, of course, personal testimonies; but they are also the individual stories by which we begin to discern patterns of a collective experience that we can comprehend as *history.* Such is the view of the modern black novelist and essayist Ralph Ellison. Ellison has argued that autobiographical works (his own *Invisible Man* or the slave narratives) both emerge from history and allow us access to it. "One of the reasons we exchange experiences," says Ellison, "is in order to discover the repetitions and coincidences which amount to a common group experience. We tell ourselves our individual stories so as to become aware of our *general* story." W. E. B. Du Bois, author of *The Souls of Black Folk* (1903) and the most prolific black scholar of the twentieth century, also saw individual and collective meanings in Douglass's *Narrative.* In his *Black Reconstruction in America* (1935), Du Bois asks the question each generation of American students and scholars should ask: "What was slavery in the United States? Just what did it mean to the owner and the owned?" Du Bois answers by asserting that the plantation legend would only be overturned by consulting the slave autobiographies. "No one can read that first thin autobiography of Frederick Douglass," he writes, "and have left many illusions about slavery . . . no amount of flowery romance and personal reminiscences of its protected beneficiaries can keep the world from knowing that slavery was a cruel, dirty, costly and inexcusable anachronism, which nearly ruined the world's greatest experiment in democracy."[27]

One of Douglass's favorite techniques was to connect his personal story to the plight of the nation, to link the Edward Coveys and Thomas Aulds in his own life to slaveholding America. He never did this more effectively than in the brilliant, bitterly ironic jeremiad "What to the Slave is the Fourth of July?" delivered in Rochester, New York, in 1852 and reprinted in this volume. In the *Narrative,* moreover, we find an intriguing link between the long chapter on the Covey fight, with its description of personal resurrection through force, and the appendix, which is an angry attack on both religious hypocrisy and the slaveholding republic, climaxing with a passage directly from Jeremiah: "Shall I not visit for these things? saith the Lord. Shall not my soul be avenged on such a nation as this?"[28] A major argument of Douglass's *Narrative,* and something he would repeat in many forms down to the Civil War, is that the "prison" of slavery housed blacks and whites, slaves and slaveholders, the entire nation in a single fate.

Douglass's *Narrative* quickly became a best-seller. Much anticipated among abolitionists, it sold five thousand copies in the first four months of publication. In August 1845 Douglass's possessive but encouraging sponsors among the New England abolitionists sent the young author on a tour of the British Isles. Britain had abolished slavery in its colonies more than a decade before, and strong ties existed between American and British abolitionists. Moreover, Douglass was still a fugitive slave, and after publishing his story and his true identity, a trip abroad might provide temporary safe haven from possible slave catchers.

His nearly twenty months out of the country were a personal and political awakening for Douglass. He took the Irish, Scottish, and British antislavery communities by storm, drew huge audiences to his speeches, and discovered environments that appeared to be devoid of the grinding racism he had encountered everywhere during his travels in America. Douglass helped finance his British tour by selling the *Narrative,* which went through nine editions and sold eleven thousand copies from 1845 to 1847. By the eve of the Civil War in 1860, approximately thirty thousand copies of the *Narrative* had been sold on two continents, and the book had been translated into both French and German editions.[29] Indeed, along with his public speeches, the *Narrative* made Frederick Douglass the most famous black person in the world.

Except for Harriet Beecher Stowe's enormously successful *Uncle Tom's Cabin* (1852), the Romantic age in America had no more popular exemplars than the narratives of fugitive slaves. Indeed, the slave autobiographies published in the 1830s and 1840s may have helped prepare the audience for Stowe's classic best-seller. The great antebellum works of Ralph Waldo Emerson, Henry David Thoreau, Walt Whitman, Herman Melville, or Margaret Fuller did not sell nearly as well as the approximately one hundred book-length slave narratives. The epic character of individuals who first *willed* their own freedom, then *wrote* the story proved irresistible to readers in the American North and in Britain. Those who would never literally see slavery could now find a literary medium through which to observe and perhaps understand it.

By attending a speech by Douglass or by reading his narrative, or those of the former fugitive slaves Harriet Jacobs, William Wells Brown, or Josiah Henson, white audiences not only encountered the heroic in form but heard or read the slave's own *voice* in substance. The abolitionist U.S. Senator Charles Sumner captured some of these sentiments in 1852, when, having read several narratives, he declared that fugitive slaves "are among the heroes of our age. Romance has no storms of more thrilling interest than theirs. Classical antiquity has preserved no examples of adventurous trial more worthy of renown."[30]

The two reviews of Douglass's work reprinted in this volume demonstrate the literary and social impact of slave narratives during the decade when the genre became an international sensation. In June 1845 the Transcendentalist Margaret Fuller found Douglass's story "so affecting" because it was the slave's "living voice." She admired Douglass's artistic abilities, urging that his work be "prized as a specimen of the powers of the Black Race." That strange but wonderful discovery—a black person who could write beautifully and compellingly—was to be celebrated. Douglass could not have asked for a better endorsement than Fuller's: "We wish that every one may read his book and see what a mind might have been stifled in bondage." Fuller had, indeed, seen to the core of Douglass's own sense of the message of his book. In 1849 Ephraim Peabody, a Boston Unitarian minister and moderate abolitionist, groused over the "extravagance and passion and rhetorical flourishes" in Douglass's language but boldly announced America's "mournful honor of adding a new department to the literature of civilization,—the autobiographies of escaped slaves." The slaves' quest for "freedom," said Peabody, kept "poetry and romance" alive, and readers of this Romantic age could find a "whole Iliad of woes" and a "modern Odyssey" in the slave narratives.[31]

Sympathetic commentators on Douglass's *Narrative* could not resist reaching for antiquity to explain the book's impact. William Lloyd Garrison, in his famous preface to the original edition (reprinted here), found in the best passages of Douglass's writing a "whole Alexandrian library of thought, feeling, and sentiment" (referring to the ancient Egyptian cultural capital at the mouth of the Nile River). In Wendell Phillips's prefatory letter, which also accompanied the original edition (also reprinted here), the famed abolitionist orator opened by recalling the "old fable of 'The Man and the Lion,' where the lion complained that he should not be so misrepresented 'when the lions wrote history.' I am glad the time has come when the 'lions write history.' "[32]

Such expressions of admiration for Douglass's *Narrative* by his white abolitionist friends and critics served as sanctions (which Douglass both welcomed and resented) for the veracity of his authorship in a world that, unfortunately, doubted black abilities. A good many people maintained that such books must have been ghostwritten, that no black person could achieve such a high intellectual level. But verifications like Phillips's were also recognitions of the central themes of slave narratives: They are at their core, as literary critic William L. Andrews has argued, stories about freedom and about the act of writing freely.[33] Thus did Douglass, who eventually grew a great mane of hair and even looked a little like a lion, represent himself and write his own history.

Just as historians have made innovative use of the slave narratives in recent years, literary critics have made analysis of them, especially Douglass's, into a veritable industry. This was not always the case; for more than a century, from the 1850s to 1960, Douglass's *Narrative* went out of print. As a model leader and writer, Douglass was not ignored by black writers and intellectuals from the 1890s to the 1930s; they appropriated him to every conceivable cause and debated whether he was the precursor or the antithesis of Booker T. Washington or W. E. B. Du Bois, the two dominant African American figures of the turn-of-the-century era. By the 1950s a genuine Douglass revival may be said to have begun among literary scholars, and through the civil rights revolution and the rediscovery of black history during the following decade, at least three new editions of the *Narrative* were published by 1968.[34]

During the 1970s and 1980s, Douglass's first autobiography emerged fully from obscurity and entered the larger American canon. The way analysis of the text became a kind of rite of passage in the burgeoning field of black literary criticism attests to the book's significance. Many insights of value to historians, as well as to all readers, have flowed from the unabated flood of literary essays on Douglass's *Narrative*. Critics have shown how the work fits many nineteenth-century literary traditions: sentimental fiction, the picaresque novel, and captivity narratives. But primarily the focus of analysis and debate has been Douglass's artful and self-conscious use of language.

Did Douglass, the seemingly self-taught writer, master the masters' language, or did that language still trap him within literary conventions, abolitionist and religious propaganda, and gendered assumptions? When read without adequate historical context and biographical background, some criticism of Douglass's *Narrative* renders the author a creature of language alone, a writer who somehow did not live or act *in* history. Feminist critics have recently opened a new avenue of analysis.[35] Douglass's virtual silence about his wife, Anna (who was a stalwart spouse, mother, and homemaker but never learned to read and write), as well as the manner in which he portrays the violence inflicted upon slave women (especially the beating of Aunt Hester in Chapter 1) have been brought under scrutiny. Douglass's quest to affirm his own "manhood," through either violence or literacy, is a persistent and revealing theme in the book. Not surprisingly, he wrote and spoke with the male values of the Victorian age. Women rarely have voices in Douglass's autobiographical writing. He was, after all, creating one essential, heroic character—himself. And, as he says in the famous sentence that announces the bloody contest with Covey: "You have seen how a man was made a slave; you shall see how a slave was made a man." Thus, drawing upon assertions of male virtue and religious metaphor, Douglass could declare his victory over the "snake" Covey to be his revival of a "sense of my own manhood" and his "glorious resurrection."[36] Just as in analyzing the text as a historical document we must be aware of how we are influenced by our own values and the events of our time, so, too, in analyzing the *Narrative* as literature, we should all be aware of how much we let issues of the present inform, or intrude upon, the texts of the past.

Some of the most persuasive criticism simply allows us to see, indeed, how effective Douglass was in using his own memory and imagination to reverse some of the allegedly fixed oppositions of antebellum America: master and slave, human and animal, black and white, slavery and freedom. Douglass ceaselessly creates his own dualisms to demonstrate that language can liberate just as easily as it can degrade or enslave the human spirit. This has much to do with why the *Narrative* garners such an enduring readership; his are the dualisms of the free mind becoming ever freer. Near the end of the book, just as he is about to announce the date of his escape from Maryland, Douglass tries to remember his sentiments. He matches the "wretchedness of slavery, and the blessedness of freedom," and declares that escape "was life and death with me."[37] Such passages are full of sentiment and pathos, but in them readers have always been able to find their own stories, their own sense of the terrible oppositions in life that require decisions which may bind or liberate them.

Autobiography is self-indulgent by definition. As the reconstruction of the personal story, it often masks the most private of sentiments in favor of constructing a public self serviceable to the present. Autobiographical memory, writes James Olney, is not "an orderly summoning up of something dead—a sort of Final Judgment on past events—but . . . a creative figuration of the living present and a summary reconstruction of how the present came to be that which it is."[38] Although Douglass left few hints as to exactly why or how he wrote his autobiographies, such present consciousness compelled him to write his story just as much as anyone else. Douglass's biographers have helped us understand how his autobiographies, though intended as public polemics, nevertheless reveal an orphan's endless quest to retrieve a "lost" and "usable" past in a life of great change, or to seek the truth about his unknown father. They have helped us notice the avoidances and silences in the *Narrative*—about his wife, women generally, and the fate of his brothers and sisters. They have helped us see that in Douglass's life there were, as William S. McFeely suggests, "private torments and horrors too deep in the well [of slavery] to be drawn up." Moreover, biographers have argued that through Douglass's writing and speaking he desperately sought a secure social identity, a sense of belonging in a country that until emancipation had defined his people out of the social contract.[39]

Like all autobiographers, Douglass sought to bring a sense of order to a life of potential chaos. As Douglass performed his story on abolitionist platforms and then took the spoken and written versions on the road in the

British Isles, he boldly served both public and private needs. The ruptures and discontinuities of a fugitive slave's life made for an awesome journey *from* slavery *to* freedom. This was perhaps America's ultimate progress narrative, and it compelled the young Douglass, lover of words as the only real weapon he had, to tell and retell his story. It was propaganda, but in a great cause; it was also an act of self-creation, a thoroughly human quest to know himself. Like those of all good autobiographers, Douglass's motives were both social and personal, and this should be no surprise. He wanted to understand himself within the world that so controlled him, and that he sought so dearly to change.

The American philosopher William James once wrote that after "long brooding" he concluded that "the one and the many" is the "most central of all philosophic problems." This is, indeed, the key to the relationship between autobiography and history. The *one* becomes the source of the individual narratives out of which we construct a sometimes coherent, sometimes conflicted, story about the *many*. The modern American writer Richard Rodriguez, himself the author of an autobiographical journey across boundaries of nationality and ethnicity, may have best captured the reasons why a fugitive slave like Douglass turned to first-person narrative. "Autobiography seems to me appropriate," writes Rodriguez, "to anyone who has suffered some startling change, a two-life lifetime; to anyone who is able to marvel at the sharp change in his life: I was there once, and now, my God, I am here! (. . . was blind but now I see.)" In Douglass's great story, he was lost and then he was found, and he would not let anyone forget it. Neither pious psalm nor pleasing history did he offer to his readers. By an intangible grace, good fortune, and heroic initiative, Douglass became free. Surely this is why he places us on that ridge overlooking the Chesapeake Bay, marveling at the "moving multitude of ships," as he imagines himself on one of their "gallant decks," speaks to us and the ships in alternating voices of anguish and triumph, pouring out his "soul's complaint," and converting it into an unforgettable image of the meaning of freedom.[40]

NOTES

[1]Frederick Douglass, *My Bondage and My Freedom* (1855; rpt. New York: Collier Books, 1969), 273. The literature on autobiography is massive, but for places to start on its relationship to personal memory and history, see James Olney, *Metaphors of Self: The Meaning of Autobiography* (Princeton: Princeton University Press, 1972); James Olney, ed., *Autobiography: Essays Theoretical and Critical* (Princeton: Princeton University Press, 1980); and Stephen Butterfield,

Black Autobiography in America (Amherst: University of Massachusetts Press, 1974). A classic, and especially self-conscious, probing of the meaning of autobiographical writing is Vladimir Nabokov, *Speak, Memory: An Autobiography Revisited* (1947; rev. ed. New York: Random House, 1966).

²Many other famous black abolitionists also escaped from the Eastern Shore of the Chesapeake in Maryland, among them Harriet Tubman, Henry Highland Garnet, and James W. C. Pennington.

³See Benjamin Quarles, *Frederick Douglass* (1948; rpt. New York: Atheneum, 1968), 4–11. On vigilance committees, see Benjamin Quarles, *Black Abolitionists* (New York: Oxford University Press, 1969), 150–67; and Jane H. Pease and William H. Pease, *They Who Would Be Free: Blacks' Search for Freedom, 1830–1861* (New York: Atheneum, 1974), 207–12.

⁴Frederick Douglass, *Narrative of the Life of Frederick Douglass, An American Slave, Written by Himself* (1845; rpt. New York: Doubleday, 1963), 114. All subsequent references are to this edition. On Douglass's discovery of *The Columbian Orator*, see Dickson J. Preston, *Young Frederick Douglass: The Maryland Years* (Baltimore: Johns Hopkins University Press, 1980), 96, 98–100.

⁵Henry Louis Gates, Jr., *Figures in Black: Words, Signs, and the Racial Self* (New York: Oxford University Press, 1987), 108.

⁶See William L. Andrews, *To Tell a Free Story: The First Century of Afro-American Autobiography, 1760–1865* (Urbana: University of Illinois Press, 1986). Andrews's persuasive argument is that the principal themes of the slave narratives were a multilayered quest for freedom, self-liberation, and the act of writing freely.

⁷"Southern Slavery and Northern Religion," two addresses delivered by Douglass in Concord, New Hampshire, 11 Feb. 1844, recorded by Nathaniel P. Rogers, in *Herald of Freedom* (Concord, N.H.), 16 Feb. 1844, in John W. Blassingame, ed., *The Frederick Douglass Papers*, vol. 1 (New Haven: Yale University Press, 1979), 26.

⁸*Narrative*, 44, 42–43.

⁹Ibid., 41.

¹⁰For the best general histories of abolitionism, see James B. Stewart, *Holy Warriors: The Abolitionists and American Slavery* (New York: Hill and Wang, 1976); and Merton Dillon, *The Abolitionists: The Growth of a Dissenting Minority* (New York: W. W. Norton, 1979). On Garrison's ideas and leadership, see John L. Thomas, *The Liberator, William Lloyd Garrison: A Biography* (Boston: Little, Brown, 1963). On Douglass's break with Garrison, see Waldo E. Martin, *The Mind of Frederick Douglass* (Chapel Hill: University of North Carolina Press, 1984), 40–46; William S. McFeely, *Frederick Douglass* (New York: W. W. Norton, 1990), 146–49, 175–76; and David W. Blight, *Frederick Douglass' Civil War: Keeping Faith in Jubilee* (Baton Rouge: Louisiana State University Press, 1989), 26–31.

¹¹*Narrative*, 13.

¹²*Narrative*, preface, xv. McFeely, *Frederick Douglass,* 115; William L. Andrews, "Introduction to the 1987 Edition," Frederick Douglass, *My Bondage and My Freedom* (Urbana: University of Illinois Press, 1987), xi–xxvi.

¹³Robert G. O'Meally, "Frederick Douglass' 1845 Narrative: The Text Was Meant to Be Preached," in Dexter Fisher and Robert B. Stepto, eds., *Afro-American Literature: The Reconstruction of Instruction* (New York: Modern Language Association, 1979), 210.

¹⁴Wilson J. Moses, *Black Messiahs and Uncle Toms: Social and Literary Manipulations of a Religious Myth* (University Park: Pennsylvania State University Press, 1982), 30–31; Andrews, *To Tell a Free Story,* 124. On the jeremiad, see Sacvan Berkovitch, *The American Jeremiad* (Madison: University of Wisconsin Press, 1978), 148–210; Blight, *Frederick Douglass' Civil War,* 105, 117–20; James H. Moorhead, *American Apocalypse: Yankee Protestants and the Civil War, 1860–1869* (New Haven: Yale University Press, 1978), 43–49; and David Howard-Pitney, "The Enduring Black Jeremiad: The American Jeremiad in Black Protest Rhetoric, from Frederick Douglass to W. E. B. Du Bois, 1841–1919," *American Quarterly* 38 (Fall 1986), 481–92.

¹⁵On Douglass's *Narrative* as spiritual autobiography, see Andrews, *To Tell a Free Story,* 123–27.

¹⁶*Narrative*, 66–67. On the nature of the Psalms, see *The Interpreter's Dictionary of the Bible,*

vol. 3 (New York: Abingdon Press, 1962), 942–58. On biblical radicalism, see Peter Linebaugh, "Jubilating; Or, How the Atlantic Working Class Used the Biblical Jubilee Against Capitalism, with Some Success," *Radical History Review* 50 (Spring 1991), 143–80. Douglass was so aware of the power and impact that the passage about the sailing ships had had on his readers that in his second autobiography he simply quoted it verbatim. See *My Bondage and My Freedom,* 219–21.

[17]Ulrich B. Phillips, *American Negro Slavery* (New York: D. Appleton, 1918); and Ulrich B. Phillips, *Life and Labor in the Old South* (Boston: Little, Brown, 1929), 219.

[18]For a rich survey of the revival of interest in slave narratives and an argument for their use by historians, see John W. Blassingame, ed., *Slave Testimony: Two Centuries of Letters, Speeches, Interviews, and Autobiographies* (Baton Rouge: Louisiana State University Press, 1977), xvii–lxv.

[19]The first modern edition was by Harvard University Press, Benjamin Quarles, ed., *Narrative of the Life of Frederick Douglass, An American Slave, Written by Himself* (Cambridge: Harvard University Press, 1960). John W. Blassingame, *The Slave Community: Plantation Life in the Antebellum South* (New York: Oxford University Press, 1972); Eugene D. Genovese, *Roll, Jordan, Roll: The World the Slaves Made* (New York: Random House, 1974); Herbert Gutman, *The Black Family in Slavery and Freedom, 1750–1925* (New York: Random House, 1976); and Lawrence W. Levine, *Black Culture and Black Consciousness: Afro-American Folk Thought from Slavery to Freedom* (New York: Oxford University Press, 1977). There are many good historiographical essays on slavery; for one of the best during the peak years of attention to this field, see David Brion Davis, "Slavery and the Post–World War II Historians," *Daedalus* 3 (Spring 1974). For a single-volume survey of slavery historiography, see Peter J. Parish, *Slavery: History and the Historians* (New York: Harper & Row, 1989).

[20]*Narrative,* 82, 84–85.

[21]*Narrative,* 54–55, 39. On Douglass and slaveholders, see Blight, *Frederick Douglass' Civil War,* 43–44, 83–88.

[22]Douglass to Thomas Auld, 3 Sept. 1848, in *The Liberator,* 22 Sept. 1848, in Philip S. Foner, *Life and Writings of Frederick Douglass,* vol. 1 (New York: International Publishers, 1950), 343. On the Douglass–Thomas Auld relationship and the inaccuracies in the letter, see Preston, *Young Frederick Douglass,* 184–87; and McFeely, *Frederick Douglass,* 40–43, 158–60.

[23]*Narrative,* 11–12, 24–26.

[24]Ibid., 47–48.

[25]Ibid., 17, 20.

[26]Ibid., 13–15; Levine, *Black Culture,* 29. Sterling Stuckey, "Through the Prism of Folklore," *Massachusetts Review* 9 (1968), 417–37; and Leon F. Litwack, *Been in the Storm So Long: The Aftermath of Slavery* (New York: Random House, 1979). Douglass also discusses the slave songs in the other two autobiographies. See *My Bondage and My Freedom,* 253–54; and *Life and Times of Frederick Douglass* (1881; rpt. New York: Collier Books, 1962), 159–60.

[27]Ralph Ellison, in a 1978 interview quoted in Charles T. Davis and Henry Louis Gates, Jr., eds., *The Slave's Narrative* (New York: Oxford University Press, 1985), xviii–xix; W. E. B. Du Bois, *Black Reconstruction in America, 1860–1880* (New York: Atheneum, 1935), 715.

[28]*Narrative,* 121. The biblical reference is Jeremiah 6:29.

[29]Davis and Gates, eds., *Slave's Narrative,* xvi; Andrews, *To Tell a Free Story,* 97–98. For more detailed sales statistics on slave narratives generally, see Charles H. Nichols, "Who Read the Slave Narratives?" *Phylon* 20 (Summer 1959), 149–62; Arna Bontemps, "The Slave Narrative: An American Genre," in *Great Slave Narratives* (Boston: Beacon Press, 1969), xvii–xix; and Marion Wilson Starling, *The Slave Narrative: Its Place in American History* (Washington, D.C.: Howard University Press, 1988), 32–39.

[30]Sumner quoted in Davis and Gates, eds., *Slave's Narrative,* xxii.

[31]Margaret Fuller, *New York Tribune,* 10 June 1845; Ephraim Peabody, *Christian Examiner,* July 1849. Both reviews are reprinted in William L. Andrews, ed., *Critical Essays on Frederick Douglass* (Boston: G. K. Hall, 1991), 21–26.

[32]*Narrative,* xv, xxi.

[33] Andrews, *To Tell a Free Story,* 103–4.

[34] For the early argument that Douglass represented the black protest tradition, see Kelly Miller, "Radicals and Conservatives," in *Race Adjustment: The Everlasting Stain* (New York: Ayer, 1908), 11–27. The revival of critical interest in Douglass can be traced to Benjamin Brawley, *The Negro in Literature and Art in the United States* (New York: Duffield, 1930); Vernon Loggins, *The Negro Author: His Development in America to 1900* (New York: Columbia University Press, 1931); and J. Saunders Redding, *To Make a Poet Black* (Chapel Hill: University of North Carolina Press, 1939). The three editions of the *Narrative* were by Harvard University Press (1960), Dolphin Books of Doubleday (1963), and Signet (1968).

[35] Some of the most important early essays on Douglass in the recent revival are Houston A. Baker, *Long Black Song* (Charlottesville: University Press of Virginia, 1973), 58–83; Albert E. Stone, "Identity and Art in Frederick Douglass' Narrative," *CLA Journal* 17 (1973), 192–213; and Robert B. Stepto, "Narration, Authentication, and Authorial Control in Frederick Douglass' Narrative of 1845"; O'Meally, "The Text Was Meant to Be Preached"; and Henry Louis Gates, Jr., "Binary Oppositions in Chapter One of *Narrative of the Life of Frederick Douglass, An American Slave, Written by Himself,*" all three in Fisher and Stepto, *Afro-American Literature,* 178–232. Two new collections of essays, literary and historical, have assembled a wide variety of work in the continuing scholarship. See Eric J. Sundquist, ed., *Frederick Douglass: New Literary and Historical Essays* (Cambridge: Cambridge University Press, 1990); and Andrews, ed., *Critical Essays.* For feminist critiques, see Deborah E. McDowell, "In the First Place: Making Frederick Douglass and the Afro-American Narrative Tradition," in Andrews, ed., *Critical Essays,* 192–214. Also see Jenny Franchot, "The Punishment of Esther: Frederick Douglass and the Construction of the Feminine," and Richard Yarborough, "Race, Violence, and Manhood: The Masculine Ideal in Frederick Douglass' 'The Heroic Slave,' " in Sundquist, ed., *Frederick Douglass,* 141–88.

[36] *Narrative,* 68, 74.

[37] Ibid., 105. On Douglass's use of dualisms and oppositions, see Gates, "Binary Oppositions," 212–32; and Andrews, *To Tell a Free Story,* 131–33.

[38] Olney, *Metaphors of Self,* 264.

[39] Peter F. Walker, *Moral Choices: Memory, Desire, and Imagination in Nineteenth Century American Abolition* (Baton Rouge: Louisiana State University Press, 1978), 209–28; McFeely, *Frederick Douglass,* 116. On Douglass's need for a social identity, see Blight, *Frederick Douglass' Civil War,* 73–78, 165–67, 187–89. On Douglass's need for reconciliation with his masters' families and his homecomings to Maryland after the Civil War, see Preston, *Young Frederick Douglass,* 159–97. On the overall importance of the autobiographies to Douglass's developing self-image, see Martin, *Mind of Frederick Douglass,* 253–84.

[40] William James, "The One and the Many," in Bruce Kuklick, ed., *Pragmatism* (Indianapolis: Hackett, 1981), 61; Richard Rodriguez, "An American Writer," in Werner Sollors, ed., *The Invention of Ethnicity* (New York: Oxford University Press, 1989), 7–8; *Narrative,* 66. On the public and private motivations in Douglass's *Narrative,* see Donald B. Gibson, "Reconciling Public and Private in Frederick Douglass's Narrative," *American Literature* 57 (1985), 551–69.

PART ONE

The Document

Editor's Note on the Text

The first edition of *Narrative of the Life of Frederick Douglass, An American Slave, Written by Himself,* published in May 1845 by the Anti-slavery Office, No. 25 Cornhill, Boston, Massachusetts, is reprinted here in its original version. The numbered notes are provided as a guide to modern readers and teachers. My aims in annotation have been fourfold: to clarify proper names, places, events, and dates, and to note factual errors when possible or relevant; to identify the rich, but not always obvious, literary allusions Douglass uses in his writing; to assist the reader in understanding the historical and intellectual contexts in which Douglass lived and wrote; and to suggest ways

Frederick Douglass, ca. 1845, when the *Narrative* was published

of understanding the place of this classic autobiography in the history of abolitionism, slavery, and the coming of the American Civil War. The selected reviews, other documents, and speeches were chosen to help create the immediate and short-term contexts in which Douglass wrote the *Narrative* and carried forth its story, in style and substance, to a world waiting, in both eagerness and anguish, to hear it.

Preface

In the month of August, 1841, I attended an anti-slavery convention in Nantucket, at which it was my happiness to become acquainted with Frederick Douglass, the writer of the following Narrative. He was a stranger to nearly every member of that body; but, having recently made his escape from the southern prison-house of bondage, and feeling his curiosity excited to ascertain the principles and measures of the abolitionists,—of whom he had heard a somewhat vague description while he was a slave,—he was induced to give his attendance, on the occasion alluded to, though at that time a resident in New Bedford.

Fortunate, most fortunate occurrence!—fortunate for the millions of his manacled brethren, yet panting for deliverance from their awful thraldom!—fortunate for the cause of negro emancipation, and of universal liberty!—fortunate for the land of his birth, which he has already done so much to save and bless!—fortunate for a large circle of friends and acquaintances, whose sympathy and affection he has strongly secured by the many sufferings he has endured, by his virtuous traits of character, by his ever-abiding remembrance of those who are in bonds, as being bound with them!—fortunate for the multitudes, in various parts of our republic, whose minds he has enlightened on the subject of slavery, and who have been melted to tears by his pathos, or roused to virtuous indignation by his stirring eloquence against the enslavers of men!—fortunate for himself, as it at once brought him into the field of public usefulness, "gave the world assurance of a MAN," quickened the slumbering energies of his soul, and consecrated him to the great work of breaking the rod of the oppressor, and letting the oppressed go free!

I shall never forget his first speech at the convention—the extraordinary emotion it excited in my own mind—the powerful impression it created upon a crowded auditory, completely taken by surprise—the applause which followed from the beginning to the end of his felicitous remarks. I think I never hated slavery so intensely as at that moment; certainly, my perception of the enormous outrage which is inflicted by it, on the godlike nature of its victims, was rendered far more clear than ever. There stood one, in physical proportion and stature commanding and exact—in intellect richly endowed—in natural eloquence a prodigy—in soul manifestly "created but a little lower than the angels"[1]—yet a slave, ay, a fugitive slave,—trembling for his safety, hardly daring to believe that on the American soil, a single white person could be found who would befriend him at all hazards, for the love of God and humanity! Capable of high attainments as an intellectual and moral being—needing nothing but a comparatively small amount of cultivation to make him an ornament to society and a blessing to his race—by the law of the land, by the voice of the people, by the terms of the slave code, he was only a piece of property, a beast of burden, a chattel personal, nevertheless![2]

A beloved friend from New Bedford prevailed on Mr. Douglass to address the convention. He came forward to the platform with a hesitancy and embarrassment, necessarily the attendants of a sensitive mind in such a novel position. After apologizing for his ignorance, and reminding the audience that slavery was a poor school for the human intellect and heart, he proceeded to narrate some of the facts in his own history as a slave, and in the course of his speech gave utterance to many noble thoughts and thrilling reflections. As soon as he had taken his seat, filled with hope and admiration, I rose, and declared that Patrick Henry, of revolutionary fame, never made a speech more eloquent in the cause of liberty, than the one we had just listened to from the lips of that hunted fugitive. So I believed at that time—such is my belief now. I reminded the audience of the peril which surrounded this self-emancipated young man at the North,—even in Massachusetts, on the soil of the Pilgrim Fathers, among the descendants of revolutionary sires; and I appealed to them, whether they would ever allow him to be carried back into slavery,—law or no law, constitution or no constitution. The response was unanimous and in thunder-tones—"NO!" "Will you succor and protect him as a brother-man—a resident of the old Bay State?" "YES!" shouted the whole mass, with an energy so startling, that the ruthless tyrants south of Mason and Dixon's line might almost have heard the mighty burst of feeling, and recognized it as the pledge of an invincible determination, on the part of those who gave it, never to betray him that wanders, but to hide the outcast, and firmly to abide the consequences.

It was at once deeply impressed upon my mind, that, if Mr. Douglass could be persuaded to consecrate his time and talents to the promotion of the anti-slavery enterprise, a powerful impetus would be given to it, and a stunning blow at the same time inflicted on northern prejudice against a colored complexion. I therefore endeavored to instil hope and courage into his mind, in order that he might dare to engage in a vocation so anomalous and responsible for a person in his situation; and I was seconded in this effort by warm-hearted friends, especially by the late General Agent of the Massachusetts Anti-Slavery Society, Mr. John A. Collins, whose judgment in this instance entirely coincided with my own. At first, he could give no encouragement; with unfeigned diffidence, he expressed his conviction that he was not adequate to the performance of so great a task; the path marked out was wholly an untrodden one; he was sincerely apprehensive that he should do more harm than good. After much deliberation, however, he consented to make a trial; and ever since that period, he has acted as a lecturing agent, under the auspices either of the American or the Massachusetts Anti-Slavery Society. In labors he has been most abundant; and his success in combating prejudice, in gaining proselytes, in agitating the public mind, has far surpassed the most sanguine expectations that were raised at the commencement of his brilliant career. He has borne himself with gentleness and meekness, yet with true manliness of character. As a public speaker, he excels in pathos, wit, comparison, imitation, strength of reasoning, and fluency of language. There is in him that union of head and heart, which is indispensable to an enlightenment of the heads and a winning of the hearts of others. May his strength continue to be equal to his day! May he continue to "grow in grace, and in the knowledge of God," that he may be increasingly serviceable in the cause of bleeding humanity, whether at home or abroad!

It is certainly a very remarkable fact, that one of the most efficient advocates of the slave population, now before the public, is a fugitive slave, in the person of Frederick Douglass; and that the free colored population of the United States are as ably represented by one of their own number, in the person of Charles Lenox Remond, whose eloquent appeals have extorted the highest applause of multitudes on both sides of the Atlantic. Let the calumniators of the colored race despise themselves for their baseness and illiberality of spirit, and henceforth cease to talk of the natural inferiority of those who require nothing but time and opportunity to attain to the highest point of human excellence.

It may, perhaps, be fairly questioned, whether any other portion of the population of the earth could have endured the privations, sufferings and horrors of slavery, without having become more degraded in the scale of humanity than the slaves of African descent. Nothing has been left undone to cripple their intellects, darken their minds, debase their moral nature, obliterate all traces of their relationship to mankind; and yet how wonderfully they have sustained the mighty load of a most frightful bondage, under which they have been groaning for centuries! To illustrate the effect of slavery on the white man,—to show that he has no powers of endurance, in such a condition, superior to those of his black brothers,—Daniel O'Connell, the distinguished advocate of universal emancipation, and the mightiest champion of prostrate but not conquered Ireland, relates the following anecdote in a speech delivered by him in the Conciliation Hall, Dublin, before the Loyal National Repeal Association, March 31, 1845. "No matter," said Mr. O'Connell, "under what specious term it may disguise itself, slavery is still hideous. *It has a natural, an inevitable tendency to brutalize every noble faculty of man.* An American sailor, who was cast away on the shore of Africa, where he was kept in slavery for three years, was, at the expiration of that period, found to be imbruted and stultified—he had lost all reasoning power; and having forgotten his native language, could only utter some savage gibberish between Arabic and English, which nobody could understand, and which even he himself found difficulty in pronouncing. So much for the humanizing influence of THE DOMESTIC INSTITUTION!" Admitting this to have been an extraordinary case of mental deterioration, it proves at least that the white slave can sink as low in the scale of humanity as the black one.

Mr. Douglass has very properly chosen to write his own Narrative, in his own style, and according to the best of his ability, rather than to employ some one else. It is, therefore, entirely his own production; and, considering how long and dark was the career he had to run as a slave,—how few have been his opportunities to improve his mind since he broke his iron fetters,—it is, in my judgment, highly creditable to his head and heart. He who can peruse it without a tearful eye, a heaving breast, an afflicted spirit,—without being filled with an unutterable abhorrence of slavery and all its abettors, and animated with a determination to seek the immediate overthrow of that execrable system,—without trembling for the fate of this country in the hands of a righteous God, who is ever on the side of the oppressed, and whose arm is not shortened that it cannot save,—must have a flinty heart, and be qualified to act the part of a trafficker "in slaves and the souls of men." I am confident that it is essentially true in all its statements; that nothing has been set down in malice, nothing exaggerated, nothing drawn from the imagination; that it comes short of the reality, rather than overstates a single fact in regard to SLAVERY AS IT IS.[3] The experience of Frederick Douglass, as a slave, was not a peculiar one; his lot was not especially a hard one; his case may be regarded as a very fair specimen of the treatment of slaves in Maryland, in which State it is conceded that they are better fed and less cruelly treated than in Georgia, Alabama, or Louisiana. Many have suffered incomparably more, while very few on the plantations have suffered less, than himself. Yet how deplorable was his situation! what terrible chastisements were inflicted upon his person! what still more shocking outrages were perpetrated upon his mind! with all his noble powers and sublime aspirations, how like a brute was he treated, even by those professing to have the same mind in them that was in Christ Jesus! to what dreadful liabilities was he continually subjected! how destitute of friendly counsel and aid, even in his greatest extremities! how heavy was the midnight of woe which shrouded in blackness the last ray of hope, and filled the future with terror and gloom! what longings after freedom took possession of his breast, and how his misery augmented, in proportion as he grew reflective and intelligent,—thus demonstrating that a happy slave is an extinct man! how he thought, reasoned, felt, under the lash of the driver, with the chains upon his limbs! what perils he encountered in his endeavors to escape from his horrible doom! and how signal have been his deliverance and preservation in the midst of a nation of pitiless enemies!

This Narrative contains many affecting incidents, many passages of great eloquence and power; but I think the most thrilling one of them all is the description Douglass gives of his feelings, as he stood soliloquizing respecting his fate, and the chances of his one day being a freeman, on the banks of the Chesapeake Bay—viewing the receding vessels as they flew with their white wings before the breeze, and apostrophizing them as animated by the living spirit of freedom. Who can read that passage, and be insensible to its pathos and sublimity? Compressed into it is a whole Alexandrian library of thought, feeling, and sentiment—all that can, all that need be urged, in the form of expostulation, entreaty, rebuke, against that crime of crimes,—making man the property of his fellow-man! O, how accursed is that system, which entombs the godlike mind of man, defaces the divine image, reduces those who by creation were crowned with glory and honor to a level with four-footed beasts, and exalts the dealer in human flesh above all that is called God! Why should its existence be prolonged one hour? Is it not evil, only evil, and that continually? What does its presence imply but the absence of all fear of God, all regard for man, on the part of the people of the United States? Heaven speed its eternal overthrow!

So profoundly ignorant of the nature of slavery are many persons, that they are stubbornly incredulous whenever they read or listen to any recital of the cruelties which are daily inflicted on its victims. They do not deny that the slaves are held as property; but that terrible fact seems to convey to their minds no idea of injustice, exposure to outrage, or savage barbarity. Tell them of cruel scourgings, of mutilations and brandings, of scenes of pollution and blood, of the banishment of all light and knowledge, and they affect to be greatly indignant at such enormous exaggerations, such wholesale misstatements, such abominable libels on the character of the southern planters! As if all these direful outrages were not the natural results of slavery! As if it were less cruel to reduce a human being to the condition of a thing, than to give him a severe flagellation, or to deprive him of necessary food and clothing! As if whips, chains, thumb-screws, paddles, bloodhounds, overseers, drivers, patrols, were not all indispensable to keep the slaves down, and to give protection to their ruthless oppressors! As if, when the marriage institution is abolished, concubinage, adultery, and incest, must not necessarily abound; when all the rights of humanity are annihilated, any barrier remains to protect the victim from the fury of the spoiler; when absolute power is assumed over life and liberty, it will not be wielded with destructive sway! Skeptics of this character abound in society. In some few instances, their incredulity arises from a want of reflection; but, generally, it indicates a hatred of the light, a desire to shield slavery from the assaults of its foes, a contempt of the colored race, whether bond or free. Such will try to discredit the shocking tales of slaveholding cruelty which are recorded in this truthful Narrative; but they will labor in vain. Mr. Douglass has frankly disclosed the place of his birth, the names of those who claimed ownership in his body and soul, and the names also of those who committed the crimes which he has alleged against them. His statements, therefore, may easily be disproved, if they are untrue.

In the course of his Narrative, he relates two instances of murderous cruelty,—in one of which a planter deliberately shot a slave belonging to a neighboring plantation, who had unintentionally gotten within his lordly domain in quest of fish; and in the other, an overseer blew out the brains of a slave who had fled to a stream of water to escape a bloody scourging. Mr. Douglass states that in neither of these instances was any thing done by way of legal arrest or judicial investigation. The Baltimore American, of March 17, 1845, relates a similar case of atrocity, perpetrated with similar impunity—as follows:—*"Shooting a Slave.*—We learn, upon the authority of a letter from Charles county, Maryland, received by a gentleman of this city, that a young man named Matthews, a nephew of General Matthews, and whose father, it is believed, holds an office at Washington, killed one of the slaves upon his father's farm by shooting him. The letter states that young Matthews had been left in charge of the farm; that he gave an order to the servant, which was disobeyed, when he proceeded to the house, *obtained a gun, and, returning, shot the servant.* He immediately, the letter continues, fled to his father's residence, where he still remains unmolested."—Let it never be forgotten, that no slaveholder or overseer can be convicted of any outrage perpetrated on the person of a slave, however diabolical it may be, on the testimony of colored witnesses, whether bond or free. By the slave code, they are adjudged to be as incompetent to testify against a white man, as though they were indeed a part of the brute creation. Hence, there is no legal protection in fact, whatever there may be in form, for the slave population; and any amount of cruelty may be inflicted on them with impunity. Is it possible for the human mind to conceive of a more horrible state of society?

The effect of a religious profession on the conduct of southern masters is vividly described in the following Narrative, and shown to be any thing but salutary. In the nature of the case, it must be in the highest degree pernicious. The testimony of Mr. Douglass, on this point, is sustained by a cloud of witnesses, whose veracity is unimpeachable. "A slaveholder's profession of Christianity is a palpable imposture. He is a felon of the highest grade. He is a man-stealer. It is of no importance what you put in the other scale."

Reader! are you with the man-stealers in sympathy and purpose, or on the side of their down-trodden victims? If with the former, then are you the foe of God and man. If with the latter, what are you prepared to do and dare in their behalf? Be faithful, be vigilant, be untiring in your efforts to break every yoke, and let the oppressed go free. Come what may—cost what it may—inscribe on the banner which you unfurl to the breeze, as your religious and political motto—"NO COMPROMISE WITH SLAVERY! NO UNION WITH SLAVE-HOLDERS!"

Wm. Lloyd Garrison[4]

Boston, May 1, 1845

Letter from Wendell Phillips, Esq.[5]

Boston, April 22, 1845

My Dear Friend:

You remember the old fable of "The Man and the Lion," where the lion complained that he should not be so misrepresented "when the lions wrote history."

I am glad the time has come when the "lions write history." We have been left long enough to gather the character of slavery from the involuntary evidence of the masters. One might, indeed, rest sufficiently satisfied with what, it is evident, must be, in general, the results of such a relation, without seeking farther to find whether they have followed in every instance. Indeed, those who stare at the half-peck of corn a week, and love to count the lashes on the slave's back, are seldom the "stuff" out of which reformers and abolitionists are to be made. I remember that, in 1838, many were waiting for the results of the West India experiment, before they could come into our ranks. Those "results" have come long ago; but, alas! few of that number have come with them, as converts. A man must be disposed to judge of emancipation by other tests than whether it has increased the produce of sugar,—and to hate slavery for other reasons than because it starves men and whips women,—before he is ready to lay the first stone of his anti-slavery life.

I was glad to learn, in your story, how early the most neglected of God's children waken to a sense of their rights, and of the injustice done them. Experience is a keen teacher; and long before you had mastered your A B C, or knew where the "white sails" of the Chesapeake were bound, you began, I see, to gauge the wretchedness of the slave, not by his hunger and want, not by his lashes and toil, but by the cruel and blighting death which gathers over his soul.[6]

In connection with this, there is one circumstance which makes your recollections peculiarly valuable, and renders your early insight the more remarkable. You come from that part of the country where we are told slavery appears with its fairest features. Let us hear, then, what it is at its best estate—gaze on its bright side, if it has one; and then imagination may task her powers to add dark lines to the picture, as she travels southward to that (for the colored man) Valley of the Shadow of Death, where the Mississippi sweeps along.

Again, we have known you long, and can put the most entire confidence in your truth, candor, and sincerity. Every one who has heard you speak has felt, and, I am confident, every one who reads your book will feel, persuaded that you give them a fair specimen of the whole truth. No one-sided portrait,—no wholesale complaints,—but strict justice done, whenever individual kindliness has neutralized, for a moment the deadly system with which it was strangely allied. You have been with us, too, some years, and can fairly compare the twilight of rights, which your race enjoy at the North, with that "noon of night" under which they labor south of Mason and Dixon's line. Tell us whether, after all, the half-free colored man of Massachusetts is worse off than the pampered slave of the rice swamps!

In reading your life, no one can say that we have unfairly picked out some rare specimens of cruelty. We know that the bitter drops, which even you have drained from the cup, are no incidental aggravations, no individual ills, but such as must mingle always and necessarily in the lot of every slave. They are the essential ingredients, not the occasional results, of the system.

After all, I shall read your book with trembling for you. Some years ago, when you were beginning to tell me your real name and birthplace, you may remember I stopped you, and preferred to remain ignorant of all. With the exception of a vague description, so I continued, till the other day, when you read me your memoirs. I hardly knew, at the time, whether to thank you or not for the sight of them, when I reflected that it was still dangerous, in Massachusetts, for honest men to tell their names! They say the fathers, in 1776, signed the Declaration of Independence with the halter about their necks. You, too, publish your declaration of freedom with danger compassing you around. In all the broad lands which the Constitution of the United States overshadows, there is no single spot,—however narrow or desolate,—where a fugitive slave can plant himself and say, "I am safe." The whole armory of Northern Law has no shield for you. I am free to say that, in your place, I should throw the MS. into the fire.

You, perhaps, may tell your story in safety, endeared as you are to so many warm hearts by rare gifts, and a still rarer devotion of them to the service of others. But it will be owing only to your labors, and the fearless efforts of those who, trampling the laws and Constitution of the country under their feet, are determined that they will "hide the outcast," and that their hearths shall be, spite of the law, an asylum for the oppressed, if, some time or other, the humblest may stand in our streets, and bear witness in safety against the cruelties of which he has been the victim.

Yet it is sad to think, that these very throbbing hearts which welcome your story, and form your best safeguard in telling it, are all beating contrary to the "statute in such case made and provided." Go on, my dear friend, till you, and those who, like you, have been saved, so as by fire, from the dark prison-house, shall stereotype these free, illegal pulses into statutes; and New

England, cutting loose from a blood-stained Union, shall glory in being the
house of refuge for the oppressed;—till we no longer merely *"hide* the
outcast," or make a merit of standing idly by while he is hunted in our midst;
but, consecrating anew the soil of the Pilgrims as an asylum for the oppressed, proclaim our *welcome* to the slave so loudly, that the tones shall
reach every hut in the Carolinas, and make the broken-hearted bondman leap
up at the thought of old Massachusetts.[7]

God speed the day!
Till then, and ever,
Yours truly,
Wendell Phillips

Frederick Douglass

Narrative of the Life of Frederick Douglass, An American Slave, Written by Himself

CHAPTER I

I was born in Tuckahoe, near Hillsborough, and about twelve miles from Easton, in Talbot county, Maryland. I have no accurate knowledge of my age, never having seen any authentic record containing it. By far the larger part of the slaves know as little of their age as horses know of theirs, and it is the wish of most masters within my knowledge to keep their slaves thus ignorant. I do not remember to have ever met a slave who could tell of his birthday. They seldom come nearer to it than planting-time, harvest-time, cherry-time, spring-time, or fall-time. A want of information concerning my own was a source of unhappiness to me even during childhood. The white children could tell their ages. I could not tell why I ought to be deprived of the same privilege. I was not allowed to make any inquiries of my master concerning it. He deemed all such inquiries on the part of a slave improper and impertinent, and evidence of a restless spirit. The nearest estimate I can give makes me now between twenty-seven and twenty-eight years of age. I come to this, from hearing my master say, some time during 1835, I was about seventeen years old.[1]

My mother was named Harriet Bailey.[2] She was the daughter of Isaac and Betsey Bailey, both colored, and quite dark. My mother was of a darker complexion than either my grandmother or grandfather.

My father was a white man.[3] He was admitted to be such by all I ever heard speak of my parentage. The opinion was also whispered that my master was my father; but of the correctness of this opinion, I know nothing; the means of knowing was withheld from me. My mother and I were separated when I was but an infant—before I knew her as my mother. It is a common custom, in the part of Maryland from which I ran away, to part children from their mothers at a very early age. Frequently, before the child has reached its twelfth month, its mother is taken from it, and hired out on some farm a considerable distance off, and the child is placed under the care of an old woman, too old for field labor. For what this separation is done, I do not know, unless it be to hinder the development of the child's affection toward its mother, and to blunt and destroy the natural affection of the mother for the child. This is the inevitable result.

I never saw my mother, to know her as such, more than four or five times in my life; and each of these times was very short in duration, and at night. She was hired by a Mr. Stewart, who lived about twelve miles from my home. She made her journeys to see me in the night, travelling the whole distance on foot, after the performance of her day's work. She was a field hand, and a whipping is the penalty of not being in the field at sunrise, unless a slave has special permission from his or her master to the contrary—a permission which they seldom get, and one that gives to him that gives it the proud name of being a kind master. I do not recollect of ever seeing my mother by the light of day. She was with me in the night. She would lie down with me, and get me to sleep, but long before I waked she was gone. Very little communication ever took place between us. Death soon ended what little we could have while she lived, and with it her hardships and suffering. She died when I was about seven years old, on one of my master's farms, near Lee's Mill. I was not allowed to be present during her illness, at her death, or burial. She was gone long before I knew any thing about it. Never having enjoyed, to any considerable extent, her soothing presence, her tender and watchful care, I received the tidings of her death with much the same emotions I should have probably felt at the death of a stranger.

Called thus suddenly away, she left me without the slightest intimation of who my father was. The whisper that my master was my father, may or may not be true; and, true or false, it is of but little consequence to my purpose whilst the fact remains, in all its glaring odiousness, that slaveholders have ordained, and by law established, that the children of slave women shall in all cases follow the condition of their mothers; and this is done too obviously to administer to their own lusts, and make a gratification of their wicked desires profitable as well as pleasurable; for by this cunning arrangement, the slaveholder, in cases not a few, sustains to his slaves the double relation of master and father.

I know of such cases; and it is worthy of remark that such slaves invariably suffer greater hardships, and have more to contend with, than others. They are, in the first place, a constant offence to their mistress. She is ever disposed to find fault with them; they can seldom do any thing to please her; she is never better pleased than when she sees them under the lash, especially when she suspects her husband of showing to his mulatto children favors which he withholds from his black slaves. The master is frequently compelled to sell this class of his slaves, out of deference to the feelings of his white wife; and, cruel as the deed may strike any one to be, for a man to sell his own children to human flesh-mongers, it is often the dictate of humanity for him to do so; for, unless he does this, he must not only whip them himself, but must stand by and see one white son tie up his brother, of but few shades darker complexion than himself, and ply the gory lash to his naked back; and if he lisp one word of disapproval, it is set down to his parental partiality, and only makes a bad matter worse, both for himself and the slave whom he would protect and defend.

Every year brings with it multitudes of this class of slaves. It was doubtless in consequence of a knowledge of this fact, that one great states-man of the south predicted the downfall of slavery by the inevitable laws of population. Whether this prophecy is ever fulfilled or not, it is nevertheless plain that a very different-looking class of people are springing up at the south, and are now held in slavery, from those originally brought to this country from Africa; and if their increase will do no other good, it will do away the force of the argument, that God cursed Ham, and therefore American slavery is right. If the lineal descendants of Ham are alone to be scriptur-ally enslaved, it is certain that slavery at the south must soon become unscriptural; for thousands are ushered into the world, annually, who, like myself, owe their existence to white fathers, and those fathers most fre-quently their own masters.[4]

I have had two masters. My first master's name was Anthony. I do not remember his first name. He was generally called Captain Anthony[5]—a title which, I presume, he acquired by sailing a craft on the Chesapeake Bay. He was not considered a rich slaveholder. He owned two or three farms, and about thirty slaves. His farms and slaves were under the care of an overseer. The overseer's name was Plummer. Mr. Plummer was a miserable drunkard, a profane swearer, and a savage monster. He always went armed with a cowskin and a heavy cudgel. I have known him to cut and slash the women's heads so horribly, that even master would be en-raged at his cruelty, and would threaten to whip him if he did not mind himself. Master, however, was not a humane slaveholder. It required extraordinary barbarity on the part of an overseer to affect him. He was a cruel man, hardened by a long life of slaveholding. He would at times seem to take great pleasure in whipping a slave. I have often been awakened at the dawn of day by the most heart-rending shrieks of an own aunt of mine, whom he used to tie up to a joist, and whip upon her naked back till she was literally covered with blood. No words, no tears, no prayers, from his gory victim, seemed to move his iron heart from its bloody purpose. The louder she screamed, the harder he whipped; and where the blood ran fastest, there he whipped longest. He would whip her to make her scream, and whip her to make her hush; and not until overcome by fatigue, would he cease to swing the blood-clotted cowskin. I remember the first time I ever witnessed this horrible exhibition. I was quite a child, but I well remember it. I never shall forget it whilst I remember any thing. It was the first of a long series of such outrages, of which I was doomed to be a witness and a participant. It struck me with awful force. It was the blood-stained gate, the entrance to the hell of slavery, through which I was about to pass. It was a most terrible spectacle. I wish I could commit to paper the feelings with which I beheld it.

This occurrence took place very soon after I went to live with my old master, and under the following circumstances. Aunt Hester went out one night,—where or for what I do not know,—and happened to be absent when my master desired her presence. He had ordered her not to go out evenings, and warned her that she must never let him catch her in company with a young man, who was paying attention to her belonging to Colonel Lloyd.[6] The young man's name was Ned Roberts, generally called Lloyd's Ned. Why master was so careful of her, may be safely left to conjecture. She was a woman of noble form, and of graceful proportions, having very few equals, and fewer superiors, in personal appearance, among the colored or white women of our neighborhood.

Aunt Hester had not only disobeyed his orders in going out, but had been found in company with Lloyd's Ned; which circumstance, I found, from what he said while whipping her, was the chief offence. Had he been a man of pure morals himself, he might have been thought interested in protecting the innocence of my aunt; but those who knew him will not suspect him of any such virtue. Before he commenced whipping Aunt Hester, he took her into the kitchen, and stripped her from neck to waist, leaving her neck, shoulders, and back, entirely naked. He then told her to cross her hands, calling her at the same time a d——d b——h. After crossing her hands, he tied them with a strong rope, and led her to a stool under a large hook in the joist, put in for the purpose. He made her get upon the stool, and tied her hands to the hook. She now stood fair for his infernal purpose. Her arms were stretched up at their full length, so that she stood upon the ends of her toes. He then said to her, "Now, you d——d b——h, I'll learn you how to disobey my orders!" and after rolling up his sleeves, he commenced to lay on the heavy cowskin, and soon the warm, red blood (amid heart-rending shrieks from her, and horrid oaths from him) came dripping to the floor. I was so terrified and horror-stricken at the sight, that I hid myself in a closet, and dared not venture out till long after the bloody transaction was over. I expected it would be my turn next. It was all new to me. I had never seen any thing like it before. I had always lived with my grandmother on the outskirts of the plantation, where she was put to raise the children of the younger women. I had therefore been, until now, out of the way of the bloody scenes that often occurred on the plantation.

CHAPTER II

My master's family consisted of two sons, Andrew and Richard; one daughter, Lucretia, and her husband, Captain Thomas Auld.[7] They lived in one house, upon the home plantation of Colonel Edward Lloyd. My master was Colonel Lloyd's clerk and superintendent. He was what might be called the overseer of the overseers. I spent two years of childhood on this plantation in my old master's family. It was here that I witnessed the bloody transaction recorded in the first chapter; and as I received my first impressions of slavery on this plantation, I will give some description of it, and of slavery as it there existed. The plantation is about twelve miles north of Easton, in Talbot county, and is situated on the border of Miles River. The principal products raised upon it were tobacco, corn, and wheat. These were raised in great abundance; so that, with the products of this and the other farms belonging to him, he was able to keep in almost constant employment a large sloop, in carrying them to market at Baltimore. This sloop was named Sally Lloyd, in honor of one of the colonel's daughters. My master's son-in-law, Captain Auld, was master of the vessel; she was otherwise manned by the colonel's own slaves. Their names were Peter, Isaac, Rich, and Jake. These were esteemed very highly by the other slaves, and looked upon as the privileged ones of the plantation; for it was no small affair, in the eyes of the slaves, to be allowed to see Baltimore.

Colonel Lloyd kept from three to four hundred slaves on his home plantation, and owned a large number more on the neighboring farms belonging to him.[8] The names of the farms nearest to the home plantation were Wye Town and New Design. "Wye Town" was under the overseership of a man named Noah Willis. New Design was under the overseership of a Mr. Town-send. The overseers of these, and all the rest of the farms, numbering over twenty, received advice and direction from the managers of the home planta-tion. This was the great business place. It was the seat of government for the whole twenty farms. All disputes among the overseers were settled here. If a slave was convicted of any high misdemeanor, became unmanageable, or evinced a determination to run away, he was brought immediately here, severely whipped, put on board the sloop, carried to Baltimore, and sold to Austin Woolfolk,[9] or some other slave-trader, as a warning to the slaves remaining.

Here, too, the slaves of all the other farms received their monthly allow-ance of food, and their yearly clothing. The men and women slaves received, as their monthly allowance of food, eight pounds of pork, or its equivalent in fish, and one bushel of corn meal. Their yearly clothing consisted of two coarse linen shirts, one pair of linen trousers, like the shirts, one jacket, one pair of trousers for winter, made of coarse negro cloth, one pair of stockings, and one pair of shoes; the whole of which could not have cost more than seven dollars. The allowance of the slave children was given to their moth-ers, or the old women having the care of them. The children unable to work in the field had neither shoes, stockings, jackets, nor trousers, given to them; their clothing consisted of two coarse linen shirts per year. When these failed them, they went naked until the next allowance-day. Children from seven to ten years old, of both sexes, almost naked, might be seen at all seasons of the year.

There were no beds given the slaves, unless one coarse blanket be con-sidered such, and none but the men and women had these. This, however, is not considered a very great privation. They find less difficulty from the want of beds, than from the want of time to sleep; for when their day's work in the field is done, the most of them having their washing, mending, and cooking to do, and having few or none of the ordinary facilities for doing either of these, very many of their sleeping hours are consumed in preparing for the field the coming day; and when this is done, old and young, male and female, married and single, drop down side by side, on one common bed,—the cold, damp floor,—each covering himself or herself with their miserable blankets; and here they sleep till they are summoned to the field by the driver's horn. At the sound of this, all must rise, and be off to the field. There must be no halting; every one must be at his or her post; and woe betides them who hear not this morning summons to the field; for if they are not awakened by the sense of hearing, they are by the sense of feeling: no age nor sex finds any favor. Mr. Severe, the overseer, used to stand by the door of the quarter, armed with a large hickory stick and heavy cowskin, ready to whip any one who was so unfortunate as not to hear, or, from any other cause, was prevented from being ready to start for the field at the sound of the horn.[10]

Mr. Severe was rightly named: he was a cruel man. I have seen him whip a woman, causing the blood to run half an hour at the time; and this, too, in the midst of her crying children, pleading for their mother's release. He seemed to take pleasure in manifesting his fiendish barbarity. Added to his cruelty, he was a profane swearer. It was enough to chill the blood and stiffen the hair of an ordinary man to hear him talk. Scarce a sentence escaped him but that was commenced or concluded by some horrid oath. The field was the place to witness his cruelty and profanity. His presence made it both the field of blood and of blasphemy. From the rising till the going down of the sun, he was cursing, raving, cutting, and slashing among the slaves of the field, in the most frightful manner. His career was short. He died very soon after I went to Colonel Lloyd's; and he died as he lived, uttering, with his dying groans, bitter curses and horrid oaths. His death was regarded by the slaves as the result of a merciful providence.

Mr. Severe's place was filled by a Mr. Hopkins.[11] He was a very different man. He was less cruel, less profane, and made less noise, than Mr. Severe. His course was characterized by no extraordinary demonstrations of cruelty. He whipped, but seemed to take no pleasure in it. He was called by the slaves a good overseer.

The home plantation of Colonel Lloyd wore the appearance of a country village. All the mechanical operations for all the farms were performed here. The shoemaking and mending, the blacksmithing, cartwrighting, coopering, weaving, and grain-grinding, were all performed by the slaves on the home plantation. The whole place wore a business-like aspect very unlike the neighboring farms. The number of houses, too, conspired to give it advantage over the neighboring farms. It was called by the slaves the *Great House Farm*. Few privileges were esteemed higher, by the slaves of the out-farms, than that of being selected to do errands at the Great House Farm. It was associated in their minds with greatness. A representative could not be prouder of his election to a seat in the American Congress, than a slave on one of the out-farms would be of his election to do errands at the Great House Farm. They regarded it as evidence of great confidence reposed in them by their overseers; and it was on this account, as well as a constant desire to be out of the field from under the driver's lash, that they esteemed it a high privilege, one worth careful living for. He was called the smartest and most trusty fellow, who had this honor conferred upon him the most frequently. The competitors for this office sought as diligently to please their overseers, as the office-seekers in the political parties seek to please and deceive the

The Lloyd plantation on the Wye River, Eastern Shore, Maryland, as it appears today. The Wye River opens into Chesapeake Bay. Douglass lived here as a slave child from summer 1824 to March 1826. This is the "Great House Farm" of the *Narrative*.

people. The same traits of character might be seen in Colonel Lloyd's slaves, as are seen in the slaves of the political parties.[12]

The slaves selected to go to the Great House Farm, for the monthly allowance for themselves and their fellow-slaves, were peculiarly enthusiastic. While on their way, they would make the dense old woods, for miles around, reverberate with their wild songs, revealing at once the highest joy and the deepest sadness. They would compose and sing as they went along, consulting neither time nor tune. The thought that came up, came out—if not in the word, in the sound;—and as frequently in the one as in the other. They would sometimes sing the most pathetic sentiment in the most rapturous tone, and the most rapturous sentiment in the most pathetic tone. Into all of their songs they would manage to weave something of the Great House Farm. Especially would they do this, when leaving home. They would then sing most exultingly the following words:—

> I am going away to the Great House Farm!
> O, yea! O, yea! O!

This they would sing, as a chorus, to words which to many would seem unmeaning jargon, but which, nevertheless, were full of meaning to themselves. I have sometimes thought that the mere hearing of those songs would do more to impress some minds with the horrible character of slavery, than the reading of whole volumes of philosophy on the subject could do.

I did not, when a slave, understand the deep meaning of those rude and apparently incoherent songs. I was myself within the circle; so that I neither saw nor heard as those without might see and hear. They told a tale of woe which was then altogether beyond my feeble comprehension; they were tones loud, long, and deep; they breathed the prayer and complaint of souls boiling over with the bitterest anguish. Every tone was a testimony against slavery, and a prayer to God for deliverance from chains. The hearing of those wild notes always depressed my spirit, and filled me with ineffable sadness, I have frequently found myself in tears while hearing them. The mere recurrence to those songs, even now, afflicts me; and while I am writing these lines, an expression of feeling has already found its way down my cheek. To those songs I trace my first glimmering conception of the dehumanizing character of slavery. I can never get rid of that conception. Those songs still follow me, to deepen my hatred of slavery, and quicken my sympathies for my brethren in bonds. If any one wishes to be impressed with the soul-killing effects of slavery, let him go to Colonel Lloyd's plantation, and, on allowance-day, place himself in the deep pine woods, and there let him, in silence, analyze the sounds that shall pass through the chambers of his soul,—and if he is not thus impressed, it will only be because "there is no flesh in his obdurate heart."[13]

I have often been utterly astonished, since I came to the north, to find persons who could speak of the singing, among slaves, as evidence of their contentment and happiness. It is impossible to conceive of a greater mistake. Slaves sing most when they are most unhappy. The songs of the slave represent the sorrows of his heart; and he is relieved by them, only as an aching heart is relieved by its tears. At least, such is my experience. I have often sung to drown my sorrow, but seldom to express my happiness. Crying for joy, and singing for joy, were alike uncommon to me while in the jaws of slavery. The singing of a man cast away upon a desolate island might be as appropriately considered as evidence of contentment and happiness, as the singing of a slave; the songs of the one and of the other are prompted by the same emotion.

CHAPTER III

Colonel Lloyd kept a large and finely cultivated garden, which afforded almost constant employment for four men, besides the chief gardener, (Mr. M'Durmond.) This garden was probably the greatest attraction of the place. During the summer months, people came from far and near—from Baltimore, Easton, and Annapolis—to see it. It abounded in fruits of almost every description, from the hardy apple of the north to the delicate orange of the south. This garden was not the least source of trouble on the plantation. Its excellent fruit was quite a temptation to the hungry swarms of boys, as well as the older slaves, belonging to the colonel, few of whom had the virtue or the vice to resist it. Scarcely a day passed, during the summer, but that some slave had to take the lash for stealing fruit. The colonel had to resort to all kinds of stratagems to keep his slaves out of the garden. The last and most successful one was that of tarring his fence all around; after which, if a slave was caught with any tar upon his person, it was deemed sufficient proof that he had either been into the garden, or had tried to get in. In either case, he was severely whipped by the chief gardener. This plan worked well; the slaves became as fearful of tar as of the lash. They seemed to realize the impossibility of touching *tar* without being defiled.

The colonel also kept a splendid riding equipage. His stable and carriage-house presented the appearance of some of our large city livery establishments. His horses were of the finest form and noblest blood. His carriage-house contained three splendid coaches, three or four gigs, besides dearborns and barouches of the most fashionable style.

This establishment was under the care of two slaves—old Barney and young Barney—father and son. To attend to this establishment was their sole work. But it was by no means an easy employment; for in nothing was Colonel Lloyd more particular than in the management of his horses. The slightest inattention to these was unpardonable, and was visited upon those, under whose care they were placed, with the severest punishment; no excuse could shield them, if the colonel only suspected any want of attention to his horses—a supposition which he frequently indulged, and one which, of course, made the office of old and young Barney a very trying one. They never knew when they were safe from punishment. They were frequently whipped when least deserving, and escaped whipping when most deserving it. Every thing depended upon the looks of the horses, and the state of Colonel Lloyd's own mind when his horses were brought to him for use. If a horse did not move fast enough, or hold his head high enough, it was owing to some fault of his keepers. It was painful to stand near the stable-door, and hear the various complaints against the keepers when a horse was taken out for use. "This horse has not had proper attention. He has not been suffi-ciently rubbed and curried, or he has not been properly fed; his food was too wet or too dry; he got it too soon or too late; he was too hot or too cold; he had too much hay, and not enough of grain; or he had too much grain, and not enough of hay; instead of old Barney's attending to the horse, he had very improperly left it to his son." To all these complaints, no matter how unjust, the slave must answer never a word. Colonel Lloyd could not brook any contradiction from a slave. When he spoke, a slave must stand, listen, and tremble; and such was literally the case. I have seen Colonel Lloyd make old Barney, a man between fifty and sixty years of age, uncover his bald head, kneel down upon the cold, damp ground, and receive upon his naked and toil-worn shoulders more than thirty lashes at the time. Colonel Lloyd had three sons—Edward, Murray, and Daniel,—and three sons-in-law, Mr. Winder, Mr. Nicholson, and Mr. Lowndes. All of these lived at the Great House Farm, and enjoyed the luxury of whipping the servants when they pleased, from old Barney down to William Wilkes, the coach-driver. I have seen Winder make one of the house-servants stand off from him a suitable distance to be touched with the end of his whip, and at every stroke raise great ridges upon his back.

To describe the wealth of Colonel Lloyd would be almost equal to describ-ing the riches of Job. He kept from ten to fifteen house-servants. He was said to own a thousand slaves, and I think this estimate quite within the truth.[14] Colonel Lloyd owned so many that he did not know them when he saw them; nor did all the slaves of the out-farms know him. It is reported of him, that, while riding along the road one day, he met a colored man, and addressed him in the usual manner of speaking to colored people on the public high-ways of the south: "Well, boy, whom do you belong to?" "To Colonel Lloyd," replied the slave. "Well, does the colonel treat you well?" "No, sir," was the ready reply. "What, does he work you too hard?" "Yes, sir." "Well, don't he give you enough to eat?" "Yes, sir, he gives me enough, such as it is."

The colonel, after ascertaining where the slave belonged, rode on; the man also went on about his business, not dreaming that he had been conversing with his master. He thought, said, and heard nothing more of the matter, until two or three weeks afterwards. The poor man was then informed by his overseer that, for having found fault with his master, he was now to be sold to a Georgia trader. He was immediately chained and handcuffed; and thus, without a moment's warning, he was snatched away, and forever sundered, from his family and friends, by a hand more unrelenting than death. This is the penalty of telling the truth, of telling the simple truth, in answer to a series of plain questions.[15]

It is partly in consequence of such facts, that slaves, when inquired of as to their condition and the character of their masters, almost universally say they are contented, and that their masters are kind. The slaveholders have been known to send in spies among their slaves, to ascertain their views and feelings in regard to their condition. The frequency of this has had the effect to establish among the slaves the maxim, that a still tongue makes a wise head. They suppress the truth rather than take the consequences of telling it, and in so doing prove themselves a part of the human family. If they have any thing to say of their masters, it is generally in their masters' favor, especially when speaking to an untried man. I have been frequently asked, when a slave, if I had a kind master, and do not remember ever to have given a negative answer; nor did I, in pursuing this course, consider myself as uttering what was absolutely false; for I always measured the kindness of my master by the standard of kindness set up among slaveholders around us. Moreover, slaves are like other people, and imbibe prejudices quite common to others. They think their own better than that of others. Many, under the influence of this prejudice, think their own masters are better than the masters of other slaves; and this, too, in some cases, when the very reverse is true. Indeed, it is not uncommon for slaves even to fall out and quarrel among themselves about the relative goodness of their masters, each contending for the superior goodness of his own over that of the others. At the very same time, they mutually execrate their masters when viewed separately. It was so on our plantation. When Colonel Lloyd's slaves met the slaves of Jacob Jepson, they seldom parted without a quarrel about their masters; Colonel Lloyd's slaves contending that he was the richest, and Mr. Jepson's slaves that he was the smartest, and most of a man. Colonel Lloyd's slaves would boast his ability to buy and sell Jacob Jepson. Mr. Jepson's slaves would boast his ability to whip Colonel Lloyd. These quarrels would almost always end in a fight between the parties, and those that whipped were supposed to have gained the point at issue. They seemed to think that the greatness of their masters was transferable to themselves. It was considered as being bad enough to be a slave; but to be a poor man's slave was deemed a disgrace indeed![16]

CHAPTER IV

Mr. Hopkins remained but a short time in the office of overseer. Why his career was so short, I do not know, but suppose he lacked the necessary severity to suit Colonel Lloyd. Mr. Hopkins was succeeded by Mr. Austin Gore, a man possessing, in an eminent degree, all those traits of character

indispensable to what is called a first-rate overseer.[17] Mr. Gore had served Colonel Lloyd, in the capacity of overseer, upon one of the out-farms, and had shown himself worthy of the high station of overseer upon the home or Great House Farm.

Mr. Gore was proud, ambitious, and persevering. He was artful, cruel, and obdurate. He was just the man for such a place, and it was just the place for such a man. It afforded scope for the full exercise of all his powers, and he seemed to be perfectly at home in it. He was one of those who could torture the slightest look, word, or gesture, on the part of the slave, into impudence, and would treat it accordingly. There must be no answering back to him; no explanation was allowed a slave, showing himself to have been wrongfully accused. Mr. Gore acted fully up to the maxim laid down by slaveholders,— "It is better that a dozen slaves suffer under the lash, than that the overseer should be convicted, in the presence of the slaves, of having been at fault." No matter how innocent a slave might be—it availed him nothing, when accused by Mr. Gore of any misdemeanor. To be accused was to be convicted, and to be convicted was to be punished; the one always following the other with immutable certainty. To escape punishment was to escape accusation; and few slaves had the fortune to do either, under the overseership of Mr. Gore. He was just proud enough to demand the most debasing homage of the slave, and quite servile enough to crouch, himself, at the feet of the master. He was ambitious enough to be contented with nothing short of the highest rank of overseers, and persevering enough to reach the height of his ambition. He was cruel enough to inflict the severest punishment, artful enough to descend to the lowest trickery, and obdurate enough to be insensible to the voice of a reproving conscience. He was, of all the overseers, the most dreaded by the slaves. His presence was painful; his eye flashed confusion; and seldom was his sharp, shrill voice heard, without producing horror and trembling in their ranks.

Mr. Gore was a grave man, and, though a young man, he indulged in no jokes, said no funny words, seldom smiled. His words were in perfect keeping with his looks, and his looks were in perfect keeping with his words. Overseers will sometimes indulge in a witty word, even with the slaves; not so with Mr. Gore. He spoke but to command, and commanded but to be obeyed; he dealt sparingly with his words, and bountifully with his whip, never using the former where the latter would answer as well. When he whipped, he seemed to do so from a sense of duty, and feared no consequences. He did nothing reluctantly, no matter how disagreeable; always at his post, never inconsistent. He never promised but to fulfill. He was, in a word, a man of the most inflexible firmness and stone-like coolness.

His savage barbarity was equalled only by the consummate coolness with which he committed the grossest and most savage deeds upon the slaves under his charge. Mr. Gore once undertook to whip one of Colonel Lloyd's slaves, by the name of Demby.[18] He had given Demby but few stripes, when, to get rid of the scourging, he ran and plunged himself into a creek, and stood there at the depth of his shoulders, refusing to come out. Mr. Gore told him that he would give him three calls, and that, if he did not come out at the third call, he would shoot him. The first call was given. Demby made no response, but stood his ground. The second and third calls were given with the same result. Mr. Gore then, without consultation or deliberation with any one, not even giving Demby an additional call, raised his musket to his face, taking deadly aim at his standing victim, and in an instant poor Demby was no more. His mangled body sank out of sight, and blood and brains marked the water where he had stood.

A thrill of horror flashed through every soul upon the plantation, excepting Mr. Gore. He alone seemed cool and collected. He was asked by Colonel Lloyd and my old master, why he resorted to this extraordinary expedient. His reply was, (as well as I can remember,) that Demby had become unmanageable. He was setting a dangerous example to the other slaves,—one which, if suffered to pass without some such demonstration on his part, would finally lead to the total subversion of all rule and order upon the plantation. He argued that if one slave refused to be corrected, and escaped with his life, the other slaves would soon copy the example; the result of which would be, the freedom of the slaves, and the enslavement of the whites. Mr. Gore's defence was satisfactory. He was continued in his station as overseer upon the home plantation. His fame as an overseer went abroad. His horrid crime was not even submitted to judicial investigation. It was committed in the presence of slaves, and they of course could neither institute a suit, nor testify against him; and thus the guilty perpetrator of one of the bloodiest and most foul murders goes unwhipped of justice, and uncensured by the community in which he lives. Mr. Gore lived in St. Michael's, Talbot county, Maryland, when I left there; and if he is still alive, he very probably lives there now; and if so, he is now, as he was then, as highly esteemed and as much respected as though his guilty soul had not been stained with his brother's blood.

I speak advisedly when I say this,—that killing a slave, or any colored person, in Talbot county, Maryland, is not treated as a crime, either by the courts or the community. Mr. Thomas Lanman,[19] of St. Michael's, killed two slaves, one of whom he killed with a hatchet, by knocking his brains out. He used to boast of the commission of the awful and bloody deed. I have heard him do so laughingly, saying, among other things, that he was the only benefactor of his country in the company, and that when others would do as much as he had done, we should be relieved of "the d——d niggers."

The wife of Mr. Giles Hick, living but a short distance from where I used to live, murdered my wife's cousin, a young girl between fifteen and sixteen years of age, mangling her person in the most horrible manner, breaking her nose and breastbone with a stick, so that the poor girl expired in a few hours afterward.[20] She was immediately buried, but had not been in her untimely grave but a few hours before she was taken up and examined by the coroner, who decided that she had come to her death by severe beating. The offence for which this girl was thus murdered was this:—She had been set that night to mind Mrs. Hick's baby and during the night she fell asleep, and the baby cried. She, having lost her rest for several nights previous, did not hear the crying. They were both in the room with Mrs. Hicks. Mrs. Hicks, finding the girl slow to move, jumped from her bed, seized an oak stick of wood by the fireplace, and with it broke the girl's nose and breastbone, and thus ended her life. I will not say that this most horrid murder produced no sensation in the community. It did produce sensation, but not enough to bring the murderess to punishment. There was a warrant issued for her arrest, but it was never served. Thus she escaped not only punishment, but even the pain of being arraigned before a court for her horrid crime.

Whilst I am detailing bloody deeds which took place during my stay on Colonel Lloyd's plantation, I will briefly narrate another, which occurred about the same time as the murder of Demby by Mr. Gore.

Colonel Lloyd's slaves were in the habit of spending a part of their nights and Sundays in fishing for oysters, and in this way made up the deficiency of their scanty allowance. An old man belonging to Colonel Lloyd, while thus engaged, happened to get beyond the limits of Colonel Lloyd's, and on the premises of Mr. Beal Bondly.[21] At this trespass, Mr. Bondly took offence, and with his musket came down to the shore, and blew its deadly contents into the poor old man.

Mr. Bondly came over to see Colonel Lloyd the next day, whether to pay him for his property, or to justify himself in what he had done, I know not. At any rate, this whole fiendish transaction was soon hushed up. There was very little said about it at all, and nothing done. It was a common saying, even among little white boys, that it was worth a half-cent to kill a "nigger," and a half-cent to bury one.

CHAPTER V

As to my own treatment while I lived on Colonel Lloyd's plantation, it was very similar to that of the other slave children. I was not old enough to work in the field, and there being little else than field work to do, I had a great deal of leisure time. The most I had to do was to drive up the cows at evening, keep the fowls out of the garden, keep the front yard clean, and run of errands for my old master's daughter, Mrs. Lucretia Auld. The most of my leisure time I spent in helping Master Daniel Lloyd in finding his birds, after he had shot them. My connection with Master Daniel was of some advantage to me. He became quite attached to me, and was a sort of protector of me. He would not allow the older boys to impose upon me, and would divide his cakes with me.

I was seldom whipped by my old master, and suffered little from any thing else than hunger and cold. I suffered much from hunger, but much more from cold. In hottest summer and coldest winter, I was kept almost naked—no shoes, no stockings, no jacket, no trousers, nothing on but a coarse tow linen shirt, reaching only to my knees. I had no bed. I must have perished with cold, but that, the coldest nights, I used to steal a bag which was used for carrying corn to the mill. I would crawl into this bag, and there sleep on the cold, damp, clay floor, with my head in and feet out. My feet have been so cracked with the frost, that the pen with which I am writing might be laid in the gashes.[22]

We were not regularly allowanced. Our food was coarse corn meal boiled. This was called *mush*. It was put into a large wooden tray or trough, and set down upon the ground. The children were then called, like so many pigs, and like so many pigs they would come and devour the mush; some with oyster-shells, others with pieces of shingle, some with naked hands, and none with spoons. He that ate fastest got most; he that was strongest secured the best place; and few left the trough satisfied.

I was probably between seven and eight years old when I left Colonel Lloyd's plantation. I left it with joy. I shall never forget the ecstasy with which I received the intelligence that my old master (Anthony) had determined to let me go to Baltimore, to live with Mr. Hugh Auld, brother to my old master's son-in-law, Captain Thomas Auld. I received this information about three days before my departure. They were three of the happiest days I ever enjoyed. I spent the most part of all these three days in the creek, washing off the plantation scurf, and preparing myself for my departure.[23]

The pride of appearance which this would indicate was not my own. I spent the time in washing, not so much because I wished to, but because Mrs. Lucretia had told me I must get all the dead skin off my feet and knees before I could go to Baltimore; for the people in Baltimore were very cleanly, and would laugh at me if I looked dirty. Besides, she was going to give me a pair of trousers, which I should not put on unless I got all the dirt off me. The thought of owning a pair of trousers was great indeed! It was almost a sufficient motive, not only to make me take off what would be called by pig-drovers the mange, but the skin itself. I went at it in good earnest, working for the first time with the hope of reward.

The ties that ordinarily bind children to their homes were all suspended in my case. I found no severe trial in my departure. My home was charmless; it was not home to me; on parting from it, I could not feel that I was leaving any thing which I could have enjoyed by staying. My mother was dead, my grandmother lived far off, so that I seldom saw her. I had two sisters and one brother, that lived in the same house with me; but the early separation of us from our mother had well nigh blotted the fact of our relationship from our memories. I looked for home elsewhere, and was confident of finding none which I should relish less than the one which I was leaving. If, however, I found in my new home hardship, hunger, whipping, and nakedness, I had the consolation that I should not have escaped any one of them by staying. Having already had more than a taste of them in the house of my old master, and having endured them there, I very naturally inferred my ability to endure them elsewhere, and especially at Baltimore; for I had something of the feeling about Baltimore that is expressed in the proverb, that "being hanged in England is preferable to dying a natural death in Ireland." I had the strongest desire to see Baltimore. Cousin Tom, though not fluent in speech, had inspired me with that desire by his eloquent description of the place. I could never point out any thing at the Great House, no matter how beautiful or powerful, but that he had seen something at Baltimore far exceeding, both in beauty and strength, the object which I pointed out to him. Even the Great House itself, with all its pictures, was far inferior to many buildings in Baltimore. So strong was my desire, that I thought a gratification of it would fully compensate for whatever loss of comforts I should sustain by the exchange. I left without a regret, and with the highest hopes of future happiness.

We sailed out of Miles River for Baltimore on a Saturday morning. I remember only the day of the week, for at that time I had no knowledge of the days of the month, nor the months of the year. On setting sail, I walked aft, and gave to Colonel Lloyd's plantation what I hoped would be the last look. I then placed myself in the bows of the sloop, and there spent the remainder of the day in looking ahead, interesting myself in what was in the distance rather than in things near by or behind.

In the afternoon of that day, we reached Annapolis, the capital of the State. We stopped but a few moments, so that I had no time to go on shore. It was the first large town that I had ever seen, and though it would look small compared with some of our New England factory villages, I thought it a wonderful place for its size—more imposing even than the Great House Farm!

We arrived at Baltimore early on Sunday morning, landing at Smith's Wharf, not far from Bowley's Wharf. We had on board the sloop a large flock of sheep; and after aiding in driving them to the slaughter-house of Mr. Curtis on Louden Slater's Hill, I was conducted by Rich, one of the hands belonging on board of the sloop, to my new home in Alliciana Street, near Mr. Gardner's ship-yard, on Fells Point.

Mr. and Mrs. Auld were both at home, and met me at the door with their little son Thomas, to take care of whom I had been given. And here I saw what I had never seen before; it was a white face beaming with the most kindly emotions; it was the face of my new mistress, Sophia Auld.[24] I wish I could describe the rapture that flashed through my soul as I beheld it. It was a new and strange sight to me, brightening up my pathway with the light of happiness. Little Thomas was told, there was his Freddy,—and I was told to take care of little Thomas; and thus I entered upon the duties of my new home with the most cheering prospect ahead.

I look upon my departure from Colonel Lloyd's plantation as one of the most interesting events of my life. It is possible, and even quite probable, that but for the mere circumstance of being removed from that plantation to Baltimore, I should have to-day, instead of being here seated by my own table, in the enjoyment of freedom and the happiness of home, writing this Narrative, been confined in the galling chains of slavery. Going to live at Baltimore laid the foundation, and opened the gateway, to all my subsequent prosperity. I have ever regarded it as the first plain manifestation of that kind providence which has ever since attended me, and marked my life with so many favors. I regarded the selection of myself as being somewhat remarkable. There were a number of slave children that might have been sent from the plantation to Baltimore. There were those younger, those older, and those of the same age. I was chosen from among them all, and was the first, last, and only choice.

I may be deemed superstitious, and even egotistical, in regarding this event as a special interposition of divine Providence in my favor. But I should be false to the earliest sentiments of my soul, if I suppressed the opinion. I prefer to be true to myself, even at the hazard of incurring the ridicule of others, rather than to be false, and incur my own abhorrence. From my earliest recollection, I date the entertainment of a deep conviction that slavery would not always be able to hold me within its foul embrace; and in the darkest hours of my career in slavery, this living word of faith and spirit of hope departed not from me, but remained like ministering angels to cheer me through the gloom.[25] This good spirit was from God, and to him I offer thanksgiving and praise.

CHAPTER VI

My new mistress proved to be all she appeared when I first met her at the door,—a woman of the kindest heart and finest feelings. She had never had a slave under her control previously to myself, and prior to her marriage she had been dependent upon her own industry for a living. She was by trade a weaver; and by constant application to her business, she had been in a good degree preserved from the blighting and dehumanizing effects of slavery. I was utterly astonished at her goodness. I scarcely knew how to behave towards her. She was entirely unlike any other white woman I had ever seen. I could not approach her as I was accustomed to approach other white ladies. My early instruction was all out of place. The crouching servility, usually so acceptable a quality in a slave, did not answer when manifested toward her. Her favor was not gained by it; she seemed to be disturbed by it. She did not deem it impudent or unmannerly for a slave to look her in the face. The meanest slave was put fully at ease in her presence, and none left without feeling better for having seen her. Her face was made of heavenly smiles, and her voice of tranquil music.

But, alas! this kind heart had but a short time to remain such. The fatal poison of irresponsible power was already in her hands, and soon commenced its infernal work. That cheerful eye, under the influence of slavery, soon became red with rage; that voice, made all of sweet accord, changed to one of harsh and horrid discord; and that angelic face gave place to that of a demon.

Very soon after I went to live with Mr. and Mrs. Auld, she very kindly commenced to teach me the A, B, C. After I had learned this, she assisted me in learning to spell words of three or four letters. Just at this point of my progress, Mr. Auld[26] found out what was going on, and at once forbade Mrs. Auld to instruct me further, telling her, among other things, that it was unlawful, as well as unsafe, to teach a slave to read. To use his own words, further, he said, "If you give a nigger an inch, he will take an ell. A nigger should know nothing but to obey his master—to do as he is told to do. Learning would *spoil* the best nigger in the world. Now," said he, "if you teach that nigger (speaking of myself) how to read, there would be no keeping him. It would forever unfit him to be a slave. He would at once become unmanageable, and of no value to his master. As to himself, it could do him no good, but a great deal of harm. It would make him discontented and unhappy." These words sank deep into my heart, stirred up sentiments within that lay slumbering, and called into existence an entirely new train of thought. It was a new and special revelation, explaining dark and mysterious things, with which my youthful understanding had struggled, but struggled in vain. I now understood what had been to me a most perplexing difficulty—to wit, the white man's power to enslave the black man. It was a grand achievement, and I prized it highly. From that moment, I understood the pathway from slavery to freedom. It was just what I wanted, and I got it at a time when I the least expected it. Whilst I was saddened by the thought of losing the aid of my kind mistress, I was gladdened by the invaluable instruction which, by the merest accident, I had gained from my master. Though conscious of the difficulty of learning without a teacher, I set out with high hope, and a fixed purpose, at whatever cost of trouble, to learn how to read. The very decided manner with which he spoke, and strove to impress his wife with the evil consequences of giving me instruction, served to convince me that he was deeply sensible of the truths he was uttering. It gave me the best assurance that I might rely with the utmost confidence on the results which, he said, would flow from teaching me to read. What he most dreaded, that I most desired. What he most loved, that I most hated. That which to him was a great evil, to be carefully shunned, was to me a great good, to be diligently sought; and the argument which he so warmly urged, against my learning to read, only served to inspire me with a desire and determination to learn. In learning to read, I owe almost as much to the bitter opposition of my master, as to the kindly aid of my mistress. I acknowledge the benefit of both.

I had resided but a short time in Baltimore before I observed a marked difference, in the treatment of slaves, from that which I had witnessed in the country. A city slave is almost a freeman, compared with a slave on the plantation.[27] He is much better fed and clothed, and enjoys privileges altogether unknown to the slave on the plantation. There is a vestige of decency, a sense of shame, that does much to curb and check those outbreaks of atrocious cruelty so commonly enacted upon the plantation. He is a desperate slaveholder, who will shock the humanity of his nonslaveholding neighbors with the cries of his lacerated slave. Few are willing to incur the odium attaching to the reputation of being a cruel master; and above all things, they would not be known as not giving a slave enough to eat. Every city slaveholder is anxious to have it known of him, that he feeds his slaves well; and it is due to them to say, that most of them do give their slaves enough to eat. There are, however, some painful exceptions to this rule. Directly opposite to us, on Philpot Street, lived Mr. Thomas Hamilton. He owned two slaves. Their names were Henrietta and Mary. Henrietta was about twenty-two years of age, Mary was about fourteen; and of all the mangled and emaciated creatures I ever looked upon, these two were the most so. His heart must be harder than stone, that could look upon these unmoved. The head, neck, and shoulders of Mary were literally cut to pieces. I have frequently felt her head, and found it nearly covered with festering sores, caused by the lash of her cruel mistress. I do not know that her master ever whipped her, but I have been an eye-witness to the cruelty of Mrs. Hamilton. I used to be in Mr. Hamilton's house nearly every day. Mrs. Hamilton used to sit in a large chair in the middle of the room, with a heavy cowskin always by her side, and scarce an hour passed during the day but was marked by the blood of one of these slaves. The girls seldom passed her without her saying, "Move faster, you *black gip!*" at the same time giving them a blow with the cowskin over the head or shoulders, often drawing the blood. She would then say, "Take that, you *black gip!*"—continuing, "If you don't move faster, I'll move you!" Added to the cruel lashings to which these slaves were subjected, they were kept nearly half-starved. They seldom knew what it was to eat a full meal. I have seen Mary contending with the pigs for the offal thrown into the street. So much was Mary kicked and cut to pieces, that she was oftener called *"pecked"* than by her name.

CHAPTER VII

I lived in Master Hugh's family about seven years. During this time, I succeeded in learning to read and write. In accomplishing this, I was compelled to resort to various stratagems. I had no regular teacher. My mistress, who had kindly commenced to instruct me, had, in compliance with the advice and direction of her husband, not only ceased to instruct, but had set her face against my being instructed by any one else. It is due, however, to my mistress to say of her, that she did not adopt this course of treatment immediately. She at first lacked the depravity indispensable to shutting me up in mental darkness. It was at least necessary for her to have some training in the exercise of irresponsible power, to make her equal to the task of treating me as though I were a brute.

My mistress was, as I have said, a kind and tender-hearted woman; and in the simplicity of her soul she commenced, when I first went to live with her, to treat me as she supposed one human being ought to treat another. In entering upon the duties of a slaveholder, she did not seem to perceive that I sustained to her the relation of a mere chattel, and that for her to treat me as a human being was not only wrong, but dangerously so. Slavery proved as injurious to her as it did to me. When I went there, she was a pious, warm, and tender-hearted woman. There was no sorrow or suffering for which she had not a tear. She had bread for the hungry, clothes for the naked, and comfort for every mourner that came within her reach. Slavery soon proved its ability to divest her of these heavenly qualities. Under its influence, the tender heart became stone, and the lamblike disposition gave way to one of tiger-like fierceness. The first step in her downward course was in her ceasing to instruct me. She now commenced to practise her husband's precepts. She finally became even more violent in her opposition than her husband himself. She was not satisfied with simply doing as well as he had commanded; she seemed anxious to do better. Nothing seemed to make her more angry than to see me with a newspaper. She seemed to think that here lay the danger. I have had her rush at me with a face made all up of fury, and snatch from me a newspaper, in a manner that fully revealed her apprehension. She was an apt woman; and a little experience soon demonstrated, to her satisfaction, that education and slavery were incompatible with each other.

From this time I was most narrowly watched. If I was in a separate room any considerable length of time, I was sure to be suspected of having a book, and was at once called to give an account of myself. All this, however, was too late. The first step had been taken. Mistress, in teaching me the alphabet, had given me the *inch,* and no precaution could prevent me from taking the *ell.*

The plan which I adopted, and the one by which I was most successful, was that of making friends of all the little white boys whom I met in the street. As many of these as I could, I converted into teachers. With their kindly aid, obtained at different times and in different places, I finally succeeded in learning to read. When I was sent to errands, I always took my book with me, and by going one part of my errand quickly, I found time to get a lesson before my return. I used also to carry bread with me, enough of which was always in the house, and to which I was always welcome; for I was much better off in this regard than many of the poor white children in our neighborhood. This bread I used to bestow upon the hungry little urchins, who, in return, would give me that more valuable bread of knowledge. I am strongly tempted to give the names of two or three of those little boys, as a testimonial of the gratitude and affection I bear them; but prudence forbids;—not that it would injure me, but it might embarrass them; for it is almost an unpardonable offence to teach slaves to read in this Christian country. It is enough to say of the dear little fellows, that they lived on Philpot Street, very near Durgin and Bailey's ship-yard. I used to talk this matter of slavery over with them. I would sometimes say to them, I wished I could be as free as they would be when they got to be men. "You will be free as soon as you are twenty-one, *but I am a slave for life!* Have not I as good a right to be free as you have?" These words used to trouble them; they would express for me the liveliest sympathy, and console me with the hope that something would occur by which I might be free.

I was now about twelve years old, and the thought of being *a slave for life* began to bear heavily upon my heart. Just about this time, I got hold of a book entitled "The Columbian Orator."[28] Every opportunity I got, I used to read this book. Among much of other interesting matter, I found in it a dialogue between a master and his slave. The slave was represented as having run away from his master three times. The dialogue represented the conversation which took place between them, when the slave was retaken the third time. In this dialogue, the whole argument in behalf of slavery was brought forward by the master, all of which was disposed of by the slave. The slave was made to say some very smart as well as impressive things in reply to his master—things which had the desired though unexpected effect; for the conversation resulted in the voluntary emancipation of the slave on the part of the master.

In the same book, I met with one of Sheridan's mighty speeches on and in behalf of Catholic emancipation.[29] These were choice documents to me. I read them over and over again with unabated interest. They gave tongue to interesting thoughts of my own soul, which had frequently flashed through my mind, and died away for want of utterance. The moral which I gained from the dialogue was the power of truth over the conscience of even a slaveholder. What I got from Sheridan was a bold denunciation of slavery, and a powerful vindication of human rights. The reading of these documents enabled me to utter my thoughts, and to meet the arguments brought forward to sustain slavery; but while they relieved me of one difficulty, they brought on another even more painful than the one of which I was relieved. The more I read, the more I was led to abhor and detest my enslavers. I could regard them in no other light than a band of successful robbers, who had left their homes, and gone to Africa, and stolen us from our homes, and in a strange land reduced us to slavery. I loathed them as being the meanest as well as the most wicked of men. As I read and contemplated the subject, behold! that very discontentment which Master Hugh had predicted would follow my learning to read had already come, to torment and sting my soul to unutterable anguish. As I writhed under it, I would at times feel that learning to read had been a curse rather than a blessing. It had given me a view of my wretched condition, without the remedy. It opened my eyes to the horrible pit, but to no ladder upon which to get out. In moments of agony, I envied my fellow-slaves for their stupidity. I have often wished myself a beast. I preferred the condition of the meanest reptile to my own. Any thing, no matter what, to get rid of thinking! It was this everlasting thinking of my condition that tormented me.[30] There was no getting rid of it. It was pressed upon me by every object within sight or hearing, animate or inanimate. The silver trump of freedom had roused my soul to eternal wakefulness. Freedom now appeared, to disappear no more forever. It was heard in every sound, and seen in every thing. It was ever present to torment me with a sense of my wretched condition. I saw nothing without seeing it, I heard nothing without hearing it, and felt nothing without feeling it. It looked from every star, it smiled in every calm, breathed in every wind, and moved in every storm.

I often found myself regretting my own existence, and wishing myself dead; and but for the hope of being free, I have no doubt but that I should have killed myself, or done something for which I should have been killed. While in this state of mind, I was eager to hear any one speak of slavery. I was a ready listener. Every little while, I could hear something about the abolitionists. It was some time before I found what the word meant. It was always used in such connections as to make it an interesting word to me. If a slave ran away and succeeded in getting clear, or if a slave killed his master, set fire to a barn, or did any thing very wrong in the mind of a slaveholder, it was spoken of as the fruit of *abolition*.[31] Hearing the word in this connection very often, I set about learning what it meant. The dictionary afforded me little or no help. I found it was "the act of abolishing;" but then I did not know what was to be abolished. Here I was perplexed. I did not dare to ask any one about its meaning, for I was satisfied that it was something they wanted me to know very little about. After a patient waiting, I got one of our city papers, containing an account of the number of petitions from the north, praying for the abolition of slavery in the District of Columbia, and of the slave trade between the States.[32] From this time I understood the words *abolition* and *abolitionist,* and always drew near when that word was spoken, expecting to hear something of importance to myself and fellow-slaves. The light broke in upon me by degrees. I went one day down on the wharf of Mr. Waters; and seeing two Irishmen unloading a scow of stone, I went, unasked, and helped them. When we had finished, one of them came to me and asked me if I were a slave. I told him I was. He asked, "Are ye a slave for life?" I told him that I was. The good Irishman seemed to be deeply affected by the statement. He said to the other that it was a pity so fine a little fellow as myself should be a slave for life. He said it was a shame to hold me. They both advised me to run away to the north; that I should find friends there, and that I should be free. I pretended not to be interested in what they said, and treated them as if I did not understand them; for I feared they might be treacherous. White men have been known to encourage slaves to escape, and then, to get the reward, catch them and return them to their masters. I was afraid that these seemingly good men might use me so; but I nevertheless remembered their advice, and from that time I resolved to run away. I looked forward to a time at which it would be safe for me to escape. I was too young to think of doing so immediately; besides, I wished to learn how to write, as I might have occasion to write my own pass. I consoled myself with the hope that I should one day find a good chance. Meanwhile, I would learn to write.

The idea as to how I might learn to write was suggested to me by being in Durgin and Bailey's ship-yard, and frequently seeing the ship carpenters, after hewing, and getting a piece of timber ready for use, write on the timber the name of that part of the ship for which it was intended. When a piece of timber was intended for the larboard side, it would be marked thus—"L." When a piece was for the starboard side, it would be marked thus—"S." A piece for the larboard side forward, would be marked thus—"L.F." When a piece was for starboard side forward, it would be marked thus—"S.F." For larboard aft, it would be marked thus—"L.A." For starboard aft, it would be marked thus—"S.A." I soon learned the names of these letters, and for what they were intended when placed upon a piece of timber in the ship-yard. I immediately commenced copying them, and in a short time was able to make the four letters named. After that, when I met with any boy who I knew could write, I would tell him I could write as well as he. The next word would be, "I don't believe you. Let me see you try it." I would then make the letters which I had been so fortunate as to learn, and ask him to beat that. In this way I got a good many lessons in writing, which it is quite possible I should never have gotten in any other way. During this time, my copy-book was the board fence, brick wall, and pavement; my pen and ink was a lump of chalk. With these, I learned mainly how to write. I then commenced and continued copying the Italics in Webster's Spelling Book, until I could make them all without looking on the book. By this time, my little Master Thomas had gone to school, and learned how to write, and had written over a number of copy-books. These had been brought home, and shown to some of our near neighbors, and then laid aside. My mistress used to go to class meeting at the Wilk Street meeting-house every Monday afternoon, and leave me to take care of the house. When left thus, I used to spend the time in writing in the spaces left in Master Thomas's copy-book, copying what he had written. I continued to do this until I could write a hand very similar to that of Master Thomas. Thus, after a long, tedious effort for years, I finally succeeded in learning how to write.

CHAPTER VIII

In a very short time after I went to live at Baltimore, my old master's youngest son Richard died; and in about three years and six months after his death, my old master, Captain Anthony, died, leaving only his son, Andrew, and daughter, Lucretia, to share his estate. He died while on a visit to see his daughter at Hillsborough. Cut off thus unexpectedly, he left no will as to the disposal of his property. It was therefore necessary to have a valuation of the property, that it might be equally divided between Mrs. Lucretia and Master Andrew. I was immediately sent for, to be valued with the other property. Here again my feelings rose up in detestation of slavery. I had now a new conception of my degraded condition. Prior to this, I had become, if not insensible to my lot, at least partly so. I left Baltimore with a young heart overborne with sadness, and a soul full of apprehension. I took passage with Captain Rowe, in the schooner Wild Cat, and, after a sail of about twenty-four hours, I found myself near the place of my birth. I had now been absent from it almost, if not quite, five years. I, however, remembered the place very well. I was only about five years old when I left it, to go and live with my old master on Colonel Lloyd's plantation; so that I was now between ten and eleven years old.

We were all ranked together at the valuation. Men and women, old and young, married and single, were ranked with horses, sheep, and swine. There were horses and men, cattle and women, pigs and children, all holding the same rank in the scale of being, and were all subjected to the same narrow examination. Silvery-headed age and sprightly youth, maids and matrons, had to undergo the same indelicate inspection. At this moment, I saw more clearly than ever the brutalizing effects of slavery upon both slave and slaveholder.

After the valuation, then came the division. I have no language to express the high excitement and deep anxiety which were felt among us poor slaves during this time. Our fate for life was now to be decided. We had no more voice in that decision than the brutes among whom we were ranked. A single word from the white men was enough—against all our wishes, prayers, and entreaties—to sunder forever the dearest friends, dearest kindred, and strongest ties known to human beings. In addition to the pain of separation, there was the horrid dread of falling into the hands of Master Andrew. He was known to us all as being a most cruel wretch,—a common drunkard, who had, by his reckless mismanagement and profligate dissipation, already wasted a large portion of his father's property. We all felt that we might as well be sold at once to the Georgia traders, as to pass into his hands; for we knew that that would be our inevitable condition,—a condition held by us all in the utmost horror and dread.

I suffered more anxiety than most of my fellow-slaves. I had known what it was to be kindly treated; they had known nothing of the kind. They had seen little or nothing of the world. They were in very deed men and women of sorrow, and acquainted with grief. Their backs had been made familiar with the bloody lash, so that they had become callous; mine was yet tender;

for while at Baltimore I got few whippings, and few slaves could boast of a kinder master and mistress than myself; and the thought of passing out of their hands into those of Master Andrew—a man who, but a few days before, to give me a sample of his bloody disposition, took my little brother by the throat, threw him on the ground, and with the heel of his boot stamped upon his head till the blood gushed from his nose and ears—was well calculated to make me anxious as to my fate. After he had committed this savage outrage upon my brother, he turned to me, and said that was the way he meant to serve me one of these days,—meaning, I suppose, when I came into his possession.[33]

Thanks to a kind Providence, I fell to the portion of Mrs. Lucretia, and was sent immediately back to Baltimore, to live again in the family of Master Hugh. Their joy at my return equalled their sorrow at my departure. It was a glad day to me. I had escaped a worse than lion's jaws. I was absent from Baltimore, for the purpose of valuation and division, just about one month, and it seemed to have been six.

Very soon after my return to Baltimore, my mistress, Lucretia, died, leaving her husband and one child, Amanda; and in a very short time after her death, Master Andrew died. Now all the property of my old master, slaves included, was in the hands of strangers,—strangers who had had nothing to do with accumulating it. Not a slave was left free. All remained slaves, from the youngest to the oldest. If any one thing in my experience, more than another, served to deepen my conviction of the infernal character of slavery, and to fill me with unutterable loathing of slaveholders, it was their base ingratitude to my poor old grandmother. She had served my old master faithfully from youth to old age. She had been the source of all his wealth; she had peopled his plantation with slaves; she had become a great grandmother in his service. She had rocked him in infancy, attended him in childhood, served him through life, and at his death wiped from his icy brow the cold death-sweat, and closed his eyes forever. She was nevertheless left a slave—a slave for life—a slave in the hands of strangers; and in their hands she saw her children, her grandchildren, and her great-grandchildren, divided, like so many sheep, without being gratified with the small privilege of a single word, as to their or her own destiny. And, to cap the climax of their base ingratitude and fiendish barbarity, my grandmother, who was now very old, having outlived my old master and all his children, having seen the beginning and end of all of them, and her present owners finding she was of but little value, her frame already racked with the pains of old age, and complete helplessness fast stealing over her once active limbs, they took her to the woods, built her a little hut, put up a little mud-chimney, and then made her welcome to the privilege of supporting herself there in perfect loneliness; thus virtually turning her out to die! If my poor old grandmother now lives, she lives to suffer in utter loneliness; she lives to remember and mourn over the loss of children, the loss of grandchildren, and the loss of great-grandchildren.[34] They are, in the language of the slave's poet, Whittier,—

> Gone, gone, sold and gone
> To the rice swamp dank and lone,
> Where the slave-whip ceaseless swings,
> Where the noisome insect stings,
> Where the fever-demon strews
> Poison with the falling dews,
> Where the sickly sunbeams glare
> Through the hot and misty air:—
>> Gone, gone, sold and gone
>> To the rice swamp dank and lone,
>> From Virginia hills and waters—
>> Woe is me, my stolen daughters![35]

The hearth is desolate. The children, the unconscious children, who once sang and danced in her presence, are gone. She gropes her way, in the darkness of age, for a drink of water. Instead of the voices of her children, she hears by day the moans of the dove, and by night the screams of the hideous owl. All is gloom. The grave is at the door. And now, when weighed down by the pains and aches of old age, when the head inclines to the feet, when the beginning and ending of human existence meet, and helpless infancy and painful old age combine together—at this time, this most needful time, the time for the exercise of that tenderness and affection which children only can exercise towards a declining parent—my poor old grandmother, the devoted mother of twelve children, is left all alone, in yonder little hut, before a few dim embers. She stands—she sits—she staggers—she falls—she groans—she dies—and there are none of her children or grandchildren present, to wipe from her wrinkled brow the cold sweat of death, or to place beneath the sod her fallen remains. Will not a righteous God visit for these things?[36]

In about two years after the death of Mrs. Lucretia, Master Thomas married his second wife. Her name was Rowena Hamilton. She was the eldest daughter of Mr. William Hamilton. Master now lived in St. Michael's. Not long after his marriage, a misunderstanding took place between himself and Master Hugh; and as a means of punishing his brother, he took me from him to live with himself at St. Michael's. Here I underwent another most painful separation. It, however, was not so severe as the one I dreaded at the division of property; for, during this interval, a great change had taken place in Master Hugh and his once kind and affectionate wife. The influence of brandy upon him, and of slavery upon her, had effected a disastrous change in the characters of both; so that, as far as they were concerned, I thought I had little to lose by the change. But it was not to them that I was attached. It was to those little Baltimore boys that I felt the strongest attachment. I had received many good lessons from them, and was still receiving them, and the thought of leaving them was painful indeed. I was leaving, too, without the hope of ever being allowed to return. Master Thomas had said he would never let me return again. The barrier betwixt himself and brother he considered impassable.

I then had to regret that I did not at least make the attempt to carry out my resolution to run away; for the chances of success are tenfold greater from the city than from the country.

I sailed from Baltimore for St. Michael's in the sloop Amanda, Captain Edward Dodson. On my passage, I paid particular attention to the direction which the steamboats took to go to Philadelphia. I found, instead of going down, on reaching North Point they went up the bay, in a north-easterly direction. I deemed this knowledge of the utmost importance. My determination to run away was again revived. I resolved to wait only so long as the offering of a favorable opportunity. When that came, I was determined to be off.

CHAPTER IX

I have now reached a period of my life when I can give dates. I left Baltimore, and went to live with Master Thomas Auld, at St. Michael's, in March, 1832. It was now more than seven years since I lived with him in the family of my old master, on Colonel Lloyd's plantation. We of course were now almost entire strangers to each other. He was to me a new master, and I to him a new slave. I was ignorant of his temper and disposition; he was equally so of mine. A very short time, however, brought us into full acquaintance with each other. I was made acquainted with his wife not less than with himself. They were well matched, being equally mean and cruel. I was now, for the first time during a space of more than seven years, made to feel the painful gnawings of hunger—a something which I had not experienced before since I left Colonel Lloyd's plantation. It went hard enough with me then, when I could look back to no period at which I had enjoyed a sufficiency. It was tenfold harder after living in Master Hugh's family, where I had always had enough to eat, and of that which was good. I have said Master Thomas was a mean man. He was so. Not to give a slave enough to eat, is regarded as the most aggravated development of meanness even among slaveholders. The rule is, no matter how coarse the food, only let there be enough of it. This is the theory; and in the part of Maryland from which I came, it is the general practice,—though there are many exceptions. Master Thomas gave us enough of neither coarse nor fine food. There were four slaves of us in the kitchen—my sister Eliza, my aunt Priscilla, Henny, and myself;[37] and we were allowed less than a half of a bushel of corn-meal per week, and very little else, either in the shape of meat or vegetables. It was not enough for us to subsist upon. We were therefore reduced to the wretched necessity of living at the expense of our neighbors. This we did by begging and stealing, whichever came handy in the time of need, the one being considered as legitimate as the other. A great many times have we poor creatures been nearly perishing with hunger, when food in abundance lay mouldering in the safe and smoke-house, and our pious mistress was aware of the fact; and yet that mistress and her husband would kneel every morning, and pray that God would bless them in basket and store!

Bad as all slaveholders are, we seldom meet one destitute of every element of character commanding respect. My master was one of this rare sort. I do not know of one single noble act ever performed by him. The leading trait in his character was meanness; and if there were any other element in his nature, it was made subject to this. He was mean; and, like most other mean men, he lacked the ability to conceal his meanness. Captain Auld was not born a slaveholder. He had been a poor man, master only of a Bay craft. He came into possession of all his slaves by marriage; and of all men, adopted slaveholders are the worst. He was cruel, but cowardly. He commanded without firmness. In the enforcement of his rules, he was at times rigid, and at times lax. At times, he spoke to his slaves with the firmness of Napoleon and the fury of a demon; at other times, he might well be mistaken for an inquirer who had lost his way. He did nothing of himself. He might have passed for a lion, but for his ears. In all things noble which he attempted, his own meanness shone most conspicuous. His airs, words, and actions, were the airs, words, and actions of born slaveholders, and, being assumed, were awkward enough. He was not even a good imitator. He possessed all the disposition to deceive, but wanted the power. Having no resources within himself, he was compelled to be the copyist of many, and being such, he was forever the victim of inconsistency; and of consequence he was an object of contempt, and was held as such even by his slaves. The luxury of having slaves of his own to wait upon him was something new and unprepared for. He was a slaveholder without the ability to hold slaves. He found himself incapable of managing his slaves either by force, fear, or fraud. We seldom called him "master;" we generally called him "Captain Auld," and were hardly disposed to title him at all. I doubt not that our conduct had much to do with making him appear awkward, and of consequence fretful. Our want of reverence for him must have perplexed him greatly. He wished to have us call him master, but lacked the firmness necessary to command us to do so. His wife used to insist upon our calling him so, but to no purpose. In August, 1832, my master attended a Methodist camp-meeting held in the Bay-side, Talbot county, and there experienced religion. I indulged a faint hope that his conversion would lead him to emancipate his slaves, and that, if he did not do this, it would, at any rate, make him more kind and humane. I was disappointed in both these respects. It neither made him to be humane to his slaves, nor to emancipate them. If it had any effect on his character, it made him more cruel and hateful in all his ways; for I believe him to have been a much worse man after his conversion than before. Prior to his conversion, he relied upon his own depravity to shield and sustain him in his savage barbarity; but after his conversion, he found religious sanction and support for his slaveholding cruelty. He made the greatest pretensions to piety. His house was the house of prayer. He prayed morning, noon, and night. He very soon distinguished himself among his brethren, and was soon made a class-leader and exhorter. His activity in revivals was great, and he proved himself an instrument in the hands of the church in converting many souls. His house was the preacher's home. They used to take great pleasure in coming there to put up; for while he starved us, he stuffed them. We have had three or four preachers there at a time. The names of those who used to come most frequently while I lived there, were Mr. Storks, Mr. Ewery, Mr. Humphry, and Mr. Hickey. I have also seen Mr. George Cookman at our house. We slaves loved Mr. Cookman. We believed him to be a good man. We thought him instrumental in getting Mr. Samuel Harrison, a very rich slaveholder, to emancipate his slaves; and by some means got the impression that he was laboring to effect the emancipation of all the slaves. When he was at our house, we were sure to be called in to prayers. When the others were there, we were sometimes called in and sometimes not. Mr. Cookman took more notice of us than either of the other ministers. He could not come among us without betraying his sympathy for us, and, stupid as we were, we had the sagacity to see it.

While I lived with my master in St. Michael's, there was a white young man, a Mr. Wilson, who proposed to keep a Sabbath school for the instruction of such slaves as might be disposed to learn to read the New Testament. We met but three times, when Mr. West and Mr. Fairbanks, both class-leaders, with many others, came upon us with sticks and other missiles, drove us off, and forbade us to meet again. Thus ended our little Sabbath school in the pious town of St. Michael's.

I have said my master found religious sanction for his cruelty. As an example, I will state one of many facts going to prove the charge. I have seen him tie up a lame young woman, and whip her with a heavy cowskin upon her naked shoulders, causing the warm red blood to drip; and, in justification of the bloody deed, he would quote this passage of Scripture—"He that knoweth his master's will, and doeth it not, shall be beaten with many stripes."[38]

Master would keep his lacerated young woman tied up in this horrid situation four or five hours at a time. I have known him to tie her up early in the morning, and whip her before breakfast; leave her, go to his store, return at dinner, and whip her again, cutting her in the places already made raw with his cruel lash. The secret of master's cruelty toward "Henny" is found in the fact of her being almost helpless. When quite a child, she fell into the fire, and burned herself horribly. Her hands were so burnt that she never got the use of them. She could do very little but bear heavy burdens. She was to master a bill of expense; and as he was a mean man, she was a constant offence to him. He seemed desirous of getting the poor girl out of existence. He gave her away once to his sister; but, being a poor gift, she was not disposed to keep her. Finally, my benevolent master, to use his own words, "set her adrift to take care of herself." Here was a recently-converted man, holding on upon the mother, and at the same time turning out her helpless child, to starve and die! Master Thomas was one of the many pious slaveholders who hold slaves for the very charitable purpose of taking care of them.

My master and myself had quite a number of differences. He found me unsuitable to his purpose. My city life, he said, had had a very pernicious effect upon me. It had almost ruined me for every good purpose, and fitted me for every thing which was bad. One of my greatest faults was that of letting his horse run away, and go down to his father-in-law's farm, which was about five miles from St. Michael's. I would then have to go after it. My reason for this kind of carelessness, or carefulness, was, that I could always get something to eat when I went there. Master William Hamilton, my master's father-in-law, always gave his slaves enough to eat. I never left there hungry, no matter how great the need of my speedy return. Master Thomas at length said he would stand it no longer. I had lived with him nine months, during which time he had given me a number of severe whippings, all to no good purpose. He resolved to put me out, as he said, to be broken; and, for this purpose, he let me for one year to a man named Edward Covey.[39] Mr. Covey was a poor man, a farm-renter. He rented the place upon which he lived, as also the hands with which he tilled it. Mr. Covey had acquired a very high reputation for breaking young slaves, and this reputation was of immense value to him. It enabled him to get his farm tilled with much less expense to himself than he could have had it done without such a reputation. Some slaveholders thought it not much loss to allow Mr. Covey to have their slaves one year, for the sake of the training to which they were subjected, without any other compensation. He could hire young help with great ease, in consequence of this reputation. Added to the natural good qualities of Mr. Covey, he was a professor of religion—a pious soul—a member and a class-leader in the Methodist church. All of this added weight to his reputation as a "nigger-breaker." I was aware of all the facts, having been made acquainted with them by a young man who had lived there. I nevertheless made the change gladly; for I was sure of getting enough to eat, which is not the smallest consideration to a hungry man.

CHAPTER X

I left Master Thomas's house, and went to live with Mr. Covey, on the 1st of January, 1833.[40] I was now, for the first time in my life, a field hand. In my new employment, I found myself even more awkward than a country boy appeared to be in a large city. I had been at my new home but one week before Mr. Covey gave me a very severe whipping, cutting my back causing the blood to run, and raising ridges on my flesh as large as my little finger. The details of this affair are as follows: Mr. Covey sent me, very early in the morning of one of our coldest days in the month of January, to the woods, to get a load of wood. He gave me a team of unbroken oxen. He told me which was the in-hand ox, and which the off-hand one. He then tied the end of a large rope around the horns of the in-hand ox, and gave me the other end of it, and told me, if the oxen started to run, that I must hold on upon the rope. I had never driven oxen before, and of course I was very awkward. I, however, succeeded in getting to the edge of the woods with little difficulty; but I had got a very few rods into the woods, when the oxen took fright, and started full tilt, carrying the cart against trees, and over stumps, in the most frightful manner. I expected every moment that my brains would be dashed out against the trees. After running thus for a considerable distance, they finally upset the cart, dashing it with great force against a tree, and threw themselves into a dense thicket. How I escaped death, I do not know. There I was, entirely alone, in a thick wood, in a place new to me. My cart was upset and shattered, my oxen were entangled among the young trees, and there was none to help me. After a long spell of effort, I succeeded in getting my cart righted, my oxen disentangled, and again yoked to the cart. I now proceeded with my team to the place where I had, the day before, been chopping wood, and loaded my cart pretty heavily, thinking in this way to tame my oxen. I then proceeded on my way home. I had now consumed one half of the day. I got out of the woods safely, and now felt out of danger. I stopped my oxen to open the woods gate; and just as I did so, before I could get hold of my ox-rope, the oxen again started, rushed through the gate, catching it between the wheel and the body of the cart, tearing it to pieces, and coming within a few inches of crushing me against the gate-post. Thus twice, in one short day, I escaped death by the merest chance. On my return, I told Mr. Covey what had happened, and how it happened. He ordered me to return to the woods again immediately. I did so, and he followed on after me. Just as I got into the woods, he came up and told me to stop my cart, and that he would teach me how to trifle away my time, and break gates. He then went to a large gum-tree, and with his axe cut three large switches, and, after trimming them up neatly with his pocket-knife, he ordered me to take off my clothes. I made him no answer, but stood with my clothes on. He repeated his order. I still made him no answer, nor did I move to strip myself. Upon this he rushed at me with the fierceness of a tiger, tore off my clothes, and lashed me till he had worn out his switches, cutting me so savagely as to leave the marks visible for a long time after. This whipping was the first of a number just like it, and for similar offences.

I lived with Mr. Covey one year. During the first six months, of that year, scarce a week passed without his whipping me. I was seldom free from a sore back. My awkwardness was almost always his excuse for whipping me. We were worked fully up to the point of endurance. Long before day we were up, our horses fed, and by the first approach of day we were off to the field with our hoes and ploughing teams. Mr. Covey gave us enough to eat, but scarce time to eat it. We were often less than five minutes taking our meals. We were often in the field from the first approach of day till its last lingering ray had left us; and at saving-fodder time, midnight often caught us in the field binding blades.

Covey would be out with us. The way he used to stand it, was this. He would spend the most of his afternoons in bed. He would then come out fresh in the evening, ready to urge us on with his words, example, and frequently with the whip. Mr. Covey was one of the few slaveholders who could and did work with his hands. He was a hard-working man. He knew by himself just what a man or a boy could do. There was no deceiving him. His work went on in his absence almost as well as in his presence; and he had the faculty of making us feel that he was ever present with us. This he did by surprising us. He seldom approached the spot where we were at work openly, if he could do it secretly. He always aimed at taking us by surprise. Such was his cunning, that we used to call him, among ourselves, "the snake." When we were at work in the cornfield, he would sometimes crawl on his hands and knees to avoid detection, and all at once he would rise nearly in our midst, and scream out, "Ha, ha! Come, come! Dash on, dash on!" This being his mode of attack, it was never safe to stop a single minute. His comings were like a thief in the night. He appeared to us as being ever at hand. He was under every tree, behind every stump, in every bush, and at every window, on the plantation. He would sometimes mount his horse, as if bound to St. Michael's, a distance of seven miles, and in half an hour afterwards you would see him coiled up in the corner of the wood-fence, watching every motion of the slaves. He would, for this purpose, leave his horse tied up in the woods. Again, he would sometimes walk up to us, and give us orders as though he was upon the point of starting on a long journey, turn his back upon us, and make as though he was going to the house to get ready; and, before he would get half way thither, he would turn short and crawl into a fence-corner, or behind some tree, and there watch us till the going down of the sun.

Mr. Covey's *forte* consisted in his power to deceive. His life was devoted to planning and perpetrating the grossest deceptions. Every thing he possessed in the shape of learning or religion, he made conform to his disposition to deceive. He seemed to think himself equal to deceiving the Almighty. He would make a short prayer in the morning, and a long prayer at night; and, strange as it may seem, few men would at times appear more devotional than he. The exercises of his family devotions were always commenced with singing; and, as he was a very poor singer himself, the duty of raising the hymn generally came upon me. He would read his hymn, and nod at me to commence. I would at times do so; at others, I would not.[41] My non-compliance would almost always produce much confusion. To show himself independent of me, he would start and stagger through with his hymn in the most discordant manner. In this state of mind, he prayed with more than ordinary spirit. Poor man! such was his disposition, and success at deceiving, I do verily believe that he sometimes deceived himself into the solemn belief, that he was a sincere worshipper of the most high God; and this, too, at a time when he may be said to have been guilty of compelling his woman slave to commit the sin of adultery. The facts in the case are these: Mr. Covey was a poor man; he was just commencing in life; he was only able to buy one slave; and, shocking as is the fact, he bought her, as he said, for *a breeder*. This woman was named Caroline. Mr. Covey bought her from Mr. Thomas Lowe, about six miles from St. Michael's. She was a large, able-bodied woman, about twenty years old. She had already given birth to one child, which proved her to be just what he wanted. After buying her, he hired a married man of Mr. Samuel Harrison, to live with him one year; and him he used to fasten up with her every night! The result was, that, at the end of the year, the miserable woman gave birth to twins. At this result Mr. Covey seemed to be highly pleased, both with the man and the wretched woman. Such was his joy, and that of his wife, that nothing they could do for Caroline during her confinement was too good, or too hard, to be done. The children were regarded as being quite an addition to his wealth.

If at any one time of my life more than another, I was made to drink the bitterest dregs of slavery, that time was during the first six months of my stay with Mr. Covey. We were worked in all weathers. It was never too hot or too cold; it could never rain, blow, hail, or snow, too hard for us to work in the field. Work, work, work, was scarcely more the order of the day than of the night. The longest days were too short for him, and the shortest nights too long for him. I was somewhat unmanageable when I first went there, but a few months of this discipline tamed me. Mr. Covey succeeded in breaking me. I was broken in body, soul, and spirit. My natural elasticity was crushed, my intellect languished, the disposition to read departed, the cheerful spark that lingered about my eye died; the dark night of slavery closed in upon me; and behold a man transformed into a brute!

Sunday was my only leisure time. I spent this in a sort of beast-like stupor, between sleep and wake, under some large tree. At times I would rise up, a flash of energetic freedom would dart through my soul, accompanied with a faint beam of hope, that flickered for a moment, and then vanished. I sank down again, mourning over my wretched condition. I was sometimes prompted to take my life, and that of Covey, but was prevented by a combination of hope and fear. My sufferings on this plantation seem now like a dream rather than a stern reality.

Our house stood within a few rods of the Chesapeake Bay, whose broad bosom was ever white with sails from every quarter of the habitable globe. Those beautiful vessels, robed in purest white, so delightful to the eye of freemen, were to me so many shrouded ghosts, to terrify and torment me with thoughts of my wretched condition. I have often, in the deep stillness of a summer's Sabbath, stood all alone upon the lofty banks of that noble bay, and traced, with saddened heart and tearful eye, the countless number of sails moving off to the mighty ocean. The sight of these always affected me powerfully. My thoughts would compel utterance; and there, with no audience but the Almighty, I would pour out my soul's complaint, in my rude way, with an apostrophe to the moving multitude of ships:—[42]

"You are loosed from your moorings, and are free; I am fast in my chains, and am a slave! You move merrily before the gentle gale, and I sadly before the bloody whip! You are freedom's swift-winged angels, that fly round the world; I am confined in bands of iron! O that I were free! O, that I were on one of your gallant decks, and under your protecting wing! Alas! betwixt me and you, the turbid waters roll. Go on, go on. O that I could also go! Could I but swim! If I could fly! O, why was I born a man, of whom to make a brute! The glad ship is gone; she hides in the dim distance. I am left in the hottest hell of unending slavery. O God, save me! God, deliver me! Let me be free! Is there any God? Why am I a slave? I will run away. I will not stand it. Get caught, or get clear, I'll try it. I had as well die with ague as the fever. I have only one life to lose. I had as well be killed running as die standing. Only think of it; one hundred miles straight north, and I am free! Try it? Yes! God helping me, I will. It cannot be that I shall live and die a slave. I will take to the water. This very bay shall yet bear me into freedom. The steamboats steered in a north-east course from North Point. I will do the same; and when I get to the head of the bay, I will turn my canoe adrift, and walk straight through Delaware into Pennsylvania. When I get there, I shall not be required to have a pass; I can travel without being disturbed. Let but the first opportunity offer, and, come what will, I am off. Meanwhile, I will try to bear up under the yoke. I am not the only slave in the world. Why should I fret? I can bear as much as any of them. Besides, I am but a boy, and all boys are bound to some one. It may be that my misery in slavery will only increase my happiness when I get free. There is a better day coming."[43]

Thus I used to think, and thus I used to speak to myself; goaded almost to madness at one moment, and at the next reconciling myself to my wretched lot.

I have already intimated that my condition was much worse, during the first six months of my stay at Mr. Covey's, than in the last six. The circumstances leading to the change in Mr. Covey's course toward me form an epoch in my humble history. You have seen how a man was made a slave; you shall see how a slave was made a man. On one of the hottest days of the month of August, 1833, Bill Smith, William Hughes, a slave named Eli, and myself, were engaged in fanning wheat.[44] Hughes was clearing the fanned wheat from before the fan, Eli was turning, Smith was feeding, and I was carrying wheat to the fan. The work was simple, requiring strength rather than intellect; yet, to one entirely unused to such work, it came very hard. About three o'clock of that day, I broke down; my strength failed me; I was seized with a violent aching of the head, attended with extreme dizziness; I trembled in every limb. Finding what was coming, I nerved myself up, feeling it would never do to stop work. I stood as long as I could stagger to the hopper with grain. When I could stand no longer, I fell, and felt as if held down by an immense weight. The fan of course stopped; every one had his own work to do; and no one could do the work of the other, and have his own go on at the same time.

Mr. Covey was at the house, about one hundred yards from the treading-yard where we were fanning. On hearing the fan stop, he left immediately, and came to the spot where we were. He hastily inquired what the matter was. Bill answered that I was sick, and there was no one to bring wheat to the fan. I had by this time crawled away under the side of the post and rail-fence by which the yard was enclosed, hoping to find relief by getting out of the sun. He then asked where I was. He was told by one of the hands. He came to the spot, and, after looking at me awhile, asked me what was the matter. I told him as well as I could, for I scarce had strength to speak. He then gave me a savage kick in the side, and told me to get up. I tried to do so, but fell back in the attempt. He gave me another kick, and again told me to rise. I again tried, and succeeded in gaining my feet; but, stooping to get the tub with which I was feeding the fan, I again staggered and fell. While down in this situation, Mr. Covey took up the hickory slat with which Hughes had been striking off the half-bushel measure, and with it gave me a heavy blow upon the head, making a large wound, and the blood ran freely; and with this again told me to get up. I made no effort to comply, having now made up my mind to let him do his worst. In a short time after receiving this blow, my head grew better. Mr. Covey had now left me to my fate. At this moment I resolved, for the first time, to go to my master, enter a complaint, and ask his protection. In order to [do] this, I must that afternoon walk seven miles; and this, under the circumstances, was truly a severe undertaking. I was exceedingly feeble; made so as much by the kicks and blows which I received, as by the severe fit of sickness to which I had been subjected. I, however, watched my chance, while Covey was looking in an opposite direction, and started for St. Michael's. I succeeded in getting a considerable distance on my way to the woods, when Covey discovered me, and called after me to come back, threatening what he would do if I did not come. I disregarded both his calls and his threats, and made my way to the woods as fast as my feeble state would allow; and thinking I might be overhauled by him if I kept the road, I walked through the woods, keeping far enough from the road to avoid detection, and near enough to prevent losing my way. I had not gone far before my little strength again failed me. I could go no farther. I fell down, and lay for a considerable time. The blood was yet oozing from the wound on my head. For a time I thought I should bleed to death; and think now that I should have done so, but that the blood so matted my hair as to stop the wound. After lying there about three quarters of an hour, I nerved myself up again, and started on my way, through bogs and briers, barefooted and bareheaded, tearing my feet sometimes at nearly every step;

and after a journey of about seven miles, occupying some five hours to perform it, I arrived at master's store. I then presented an appearance enough to affect any but a heart of iron. From the crown of my head to my feet, I was covered with blood. My hair was all clotted with dust and blood; my shirt was stiff with blood. My legs and feet were torn in sundry places with briers and thorns, and were also covered with blood. I suppose I looked like a man who had escaped a den of wild beasts, and barely escaped them. In this state I appeared before my master, humbly entreating him to interpose his authority for my protection. I told him all the circumstances as well as I could, and it seemed, as I spoke, at times to affect him. He would then walk the floor, and seek to justify Covey by saying he expected I deserved it. He asked me what I wanted. I told him, to let me get a new home; that as sure as I lived with Mr. Covey again, I should live with but to die with him; that Covey would surely kill me; he was in a fair way for it. Master Thomas ridiculed the idea that there was any danger of Mr. Covey's killing me, and said that he knew Mr. Covey; that he was a good man, and that he could not think of taking me from him; that, should he do so, he would lose the whole year's wages; that I belonged to Mr. Covey for one year, and that I must go back to him, come what might; and that I must not trouble him with any more stories, or that he would himself *get hold of me*. After threatening me thus, he gave me a very large dose of salts, telling me that I might remain in St. Michael's that night, (it being quite late,) but that I must be off back to Mr. Covey's early in the morning; and that if I did not, he would *get hold of me*, which meant that he would whip me. I remained all night, and, according to his orders, I started off to Covey's in the morning, (Saturday morning,) wearied in body and broken in spirit. I got no supper that night, or breakfast that morning. I reached Covey's about nine o'clock; and just as I was getting over the fence that divided Mrs. Kemp's fields from ours, out ran Covey with his cowskin, to give me another whipping. Before he could reach me, I succeeded in getting to the cornfield; and as the corn was very high, it afforded me the means of hiding. He seemed very angry, and searched for me a long time. My behavior was altogether unaccountable. He finally gave up the chase, thinking, I suppose, that I must come home for something to eat; he would give himself no further trouble in looking for me. I spent that day mostly in the woods, having the alternative before me,—to go home and be whipped to death, or stay in the woods and be starved to death. That night, I fell in with Sandy Jenkins, a slave with whom I was somewhat acquainted.[45] Sandy had a free wife who lived about four miles from Mr. Covey's; and it being Saturday, he was on his way to see her. I told him my circumstances, and he very kindly invited me to go home with him. I went home with him, and talked this whole matter over, and got his advice as to what course it was best for me to pursue. I found Sandy an old adviser. He told me, with great solemnity, I must go back to Covey; but that before I went, I must go with him into another part of the woods, where there was a certain *root,* which, if I would take some of it with me, carrying it *always on my right side,* would render it impossible for Mr. Covey, or any other white man, to whip me. He said he had carried it for years; and since he had done so, he had never received a blow, and never expected to while he carried it. I at first rejected the idea, that the simple carrying of a root in my pocket would have any such effect as he had said, and was not disposed to take it; but Sandy impressed the necessity with much earnestness, telling me it could do no harm, if it did no good. To please him, I at length took the root, and, according to his direction, carried it upon my right side. This was Sunday morning. I immediately started for home; and upon entering the yard gate, out came Mr. Covey on his way to meeting. He spoke to me very kindly, made me drive the pigs from a lot near by, and passed on towards the church. Now, this singular conduct of Mr. Covey really made me begin to think that there was something in the *root* which Sandy had given me; and had it been on any other day than Sunday, I could have attributed the conduct to no other cause than the influence of that root; and as it was, I was half inclined to think the *root* to be something more than I at first had taken it to be. All went well till Monday morning. On this morning, the virtue of the *root* was fully tested. Long before daylight, I was called to go and rub, curry, and feed, the horses. I obeyed, and was glad to obey. But whilst thus engaged, whilst in the act of throwing down some blades from the loft, Mr. Covey entered the stable with a long rope; and just as I was half out of the loft, he caught hold of my legs, and was about tying me. As soon as I found what he was up to, I gave a sudden spring, and as I did so, he holding to my legs, I was brought sprawling on the stable floor. Mr. Covey seemed now to think he had me, and could do what he pleased; but at this moment—from whence came the spirit I don't know—I resolved to fight; and, suiting my action to the resolution, I seized Covey hard by the throat; and as I did so, I rose. He held on to me, and I to him. My resistance was so entirely unexpected, that Covey seemed taken all aback. He trembled like a leaf. This gave me assurance, and I held him uneasy, causing the blood to run where I touched him with the ends of my fingers. Mr. Covey soon called out to Hughes for help. Hughes came, and, while Covey held me, attempting to tie my right hand. While he was in the act of doing so, I watched my chance, and gave him a heavy kick close under the ribs. This kick fairly sickened Hughes, so that he left me in the hands of Mr. Covey. This kick had the effect of not only weakening Hughes, but Covey also. When he saw Hughes bending over with pain, his courage quailed. He asked me if I meant to persist in my resistance. I told him I did, come what might; that he had used me like a brute for six months, and that I was determined to be used so no longer. With that, he strove to drag me to a stick that was lying just out of the stable door. He meant to knock me down. But just as he was leaning over to get the stick, I seized him with both hands by his collar, and brought him by a sudden snatch to the ground. By this time, Bill came. Covey called upon him for assistance. Bill wanted to know what he could do. Covey said, "Take hold of him, take hold of him!" Bill said his master hired him out to work, and not to help to whip me; so he left Covey and myself to fight our own battle out. We were at it for nearly two hours. Covey at length let me go, puffing and blowing at a great rate, saying that if I had not resisted, he would not have whipped me half so much. The truth was, that he had not whipped me at all. I considered him as getting entirely the worst end of the bargain; for he had drawn no blood from me, but I had from him. The whole six months afterwards, that I spent with Mr. Covey, he never laid the weight of his finger upon me in anger. He would occasionally say, he didn't want to get hold of me again. "No," thought I, "you need not; for you will come off worse than you did before."

This battle with Mr. Covey was the turning-point in my career as a slave. It rekindled the few expiring embers of freedom, and revived within me a sense of my own manhood. It recalled the departed self-confidence, and inspired me again with a determination to be free. The gratification afforded by the triumph was a full compensation for whatever else might follow, even death itself. He only can understand the deep satisfaction which I experienced, who has himself repelled by force the bloody arm of slavery. I felt as I never felt before. It was a glorious resurrection, from the tomb of slavery, to the heaven of freedom. My long-crushed spirit rose, cowardice departed, bold defiance took its place; and I now resolved that, however long I might remain a slave in form, the day had passed forever when I could be a slave in fact. I did not hesitate to let it be known of me, that the white man who expected to succeed in whipping, must also succeed in killing me.

From this time I was never again what might be called fairly whipped, though I remained a slave four years afterwards. I had several fights, but was never whipped.

It was for a long time a matter of surprise to me why Mr. Covey did not immediately have me taken by the constable to the whipping-post, and there regularly whipped for the crime of raising my hand against a white man in defence of myself. And the only explanation I can now think of does not entirely satisfy me; but such as it is, I will give it. Mr. Covey enjoyed the most unbounded reputation for being a first-rate overseer and negro-breaker.[46] It was of considerable importance to him. That reputation was at stake; and had he sent me—a boy about sixteen years old—to the public whipping-post, his reputation would have been lost; so, to save his reputation, he suffered me to go unpunished.

My term of actual service to Mr. Edward Covey ended on Christmas day, 1833. The days between Christmas and New Year's day are allowed as holidays; and, accordingly, we were not required to perform any labor, more than to feed and take care of the stock. This time we regarded as our own, by the grace of our masters; and we therefore used or abused it nearly as we pleased. Those of us who had families at a distance, were generally allowed to spend the whole six days in their society. This time, however, was spent in various ways. The staid, sober, thinking and industrious ones of our number would employ themselves in making corn-brooms, mats, horse-collars, and baskets; and another class of us would spend the time in hunting opossums, hares, and coons. But by far the larger part engaged in such sports and merriments as playing ball, wrestling, running foot-races, fid-dling, dancing, and drinking whisky; and this latter mode of spending the time was by far the most agreeable to the feelings of our masters. A slave who would work during the holidays was considered by our masters as scarcely deserving them. He was regarded as one who rejected the favor of his master. It was deemed a disgrace not to get drunk at Christmas; and he was regarded as lazy indeed, who had not provided himself with the neces-sary means, during the year, to get whisky enough to last him through Christmas.

From what I know of the effect of these holidays upon the slave, I believe them to be among the most effective means in the hands of the slaveholder in keeping down the spirit of insurrection. Were the slaveholders at once to abandon this practice, I have not the slightest doubt it would lead to an immediate insurrection among the slaves. These holidays serve as conduc-tors, or safety-valves, to carry off the rebellious spirit of enslaved humanity. But for these, the slave would be forced up to the wildest desperation; and woe betide the slaveholder, the day he ventures to remove or hinder the operation of those conductors! I warn him that, in such an event, a spirit will go forth in their midst, more to be dreaded than the most appalling earth-quake.

The holidays are part and parcel of the gross fraud, wrong, and in-humanity of slavery. They are professedly a custom established by the benevolence of the slaveholders; but I undertake to say, it is the result of selfishness, and one of the grossest frauds committed upon the down-trodden slave. They do not give the slaves this time because they would not like to have their work during its continuance, but because they know it would be unsafe to deprive them of it. This will be seen by the fact, that the slaveholders like to have their slaves spend those days just in such a manner as to make them as glad of their ending as of their beginning. Their object seems to be, to disgust their slaves with freedom, by plunging them into the lowest depths of dissipation. For instance, the slaveholders not only like to see the slave drink of his own accord, but will adopt various plans to make him drunk. One plan is, to make bets on their slaves, as to who can drink the most whisky without getting drunk; and in this way they succeed in getting whole multitudes to drink to excess. Thus, when the slave asks for virtuous freedom, the cunning slaveholder, knowing his ignorance, cheats him with a dose of vicious dissipation, artfully labelled with the name of liberty. The most of us used to drink it down, and the result was just what might be supposed: many of us were led to think that there was little to choose between liberty and slavery. We felt, and very properly too, that we had almost as well be slaves to man as to rum. So, when the holidays ended, we staggered up from the filth of our wallowing, took a long breath, and marched to the field,—feeling, upon the whole, rather glad to go, from what our master had deceived us into a belief was freedom, back to the arms of slavery.

I have said that this mode of treatment is a part of the whole system of fraud and inhumanity of slavery. It is so. The mode here adopted to disgust the slave with freedom, by allowing him to see only the abuse of it, is carried out in other things. For instance, a slave loves molasses; he steals some. His master, in many cases, goes off to town, and buys a large quantity; he returns, takes his whip, and commands the slave to eat the molasses, until the poor fellow is made sick at the very mention of it. The same mode is sometimes adopted to make the slaves refrain from asking for more food than their regular allowance. A slave runs through his allowance, and applies for more. His master is enraged at him; but, not willing to send him off without food, gives him more than is necessary, and compels him to eat it within a given time. Then, if he complains that he cannot eat it, he is said to be satisfied neither full or fasting, and is whipped for being hard to please! I have an abundance of such illustrations of the same principle, drawn from my own observation, but think the cases I have cited sufficient. The practice is a very common one.[47]

On the first of January, 1834, I left Mr. Covey, and went to live with Mr. William Freeland, who lived about three miles from St. Michael's.[48] I soon found Mr. Freeland a very different man from Mr. Covey. Though not rich, he was what would be called an educated southern gentleman. Mr. Covey, as I have shown, was a well-trained negro-breaker and slavedriver. The former (slaveholder though he was) seemed to possess some regard for honor, some reverence for justice, and some respect for humanity. The latter seemed totally insensible to all such sentiments. Mr. Freeland had many of the faults peculiar to slaveholders, such as being very passionate and fretful; but I must do him the justice to say, that he was exceedingly free from those degrading vices to which Mr. Covey was constantly addicted. The one was open and frank, and we always knew where to find him. The other was a most artful deceiver, and could be understood only by such as were skilful enough to detect his cunningly-devised frauds. Another advantage I gained in my new master was, he made no pretensions to, or profession of, religion; and this, in my opinion, was truly a great advantage. I assert most unhesitatingly, that the religion of the south is a mere covering for the most horrid crimes,—a justifier of the most appalling barbarity,—a sanctifier of the most hateful frauds,—and a dark shelter under which the darkest, foulest, grossest, and most infernal deeds of slaveholders find the strongest protection. Were I to be again reduced to the chains of slavery, next to that enslavement, I should regard being the slave of a religious master the greatest calamity that could befall me. For of all slaveholders with whom I have ever met, religious slaveholders are the worst. I have ever found them the meanest and basest, the most cruel and cowardly, of all others. It was my unhappy lot not only to belong to a religious slaveholder, but to live in a community of such religionists. Very near Mr. Freeland lived the Rev. Daniel Weeden, and in the same neighborhood lived the Rev. Rigby Hopkins.[49] These were members and ministers in the Reformed Methodist Church. Mr. Weeden owned, among others, a woman slave, whose name I have forgotten. This woman's back, for weeks, was kept literally raw, made so by the lash of this merciless, *religious* wretch. He used to hire hands. His maxim was, Behave well or behave ill, it is the duty of a master occasionally to whip a slave, to remind him of his master's authority. Such was his theory, and such his practice.

Mr. Hopkins was even worse than Mr. Weeden. His chief boast was his ability to manage slaves. The peculiar feature of his government was that of whipping slaves in advance of deserving it. He always managed to have one or more of his slaves to whip every Monday morning. He did this to alarm their fears, and strike terror into those who escaped. His plan was to whip for the smallest offences, to prevent the commission of large ones. Mr. Hopkins could always find some excuse for whipping a slave. It would astonish one, unaccustomed to a slaveholding life, to see with what wonderful ease a slaveholder can find things, of which to make occasion to whip a slave. A mere look, word, or motion,—a mistake, accident, or want of power,—are all matters for which a slave may be whipped at any time. Does a slave look dissatisfied? It is said, he has the devil in him, and it must be whipped out. Does he speak loudly when spoken to by his master? Then he

is getting high-minded, and should be taken down a button-hole lower. Does he forget to pull off his hat at the approach of a white person? Then he is wanting in reverence, and should be whipped for it. Does he ever venture to vindicate his conduct, when censured for it? Then he is guilty of impudence,—one of the greatest crimes of which a slave can be guilty. Does he ever venture to suggest a different mode of doing things from that pointed out by his master? He is indeed presumptuous, and getting above himself; and nothing less than a flogging will do for him. Does he, while ploughing, break a plough,—or, while hoeing, break a hoe? It is owing to his carelessness, and for it a slave must always be whipped. Mr. Hopkins could always find something of this sort to justify the use of the lash, and he seldom failed to embrace such opportunities. There was not a man in the whole county, with whom the slaves who had the getting their own home, would not prefer to live, rather than with this Rev. Mr. Hopkins. And yet there was not a man any where round, who made higher professions of religion, or was more active in revivals,—more attentive to the class, love-feast, prayer and preaching meetings, or more devotional in his family,—that prayed earlier, later, louder, and longer,—than this same reverend slave-driver, Rigby Hopkins.

But to return to Mr. Freeland, and to my experience while in his employment. He, like Mr. Covey, gave us enough to eat; but, unlike Mr. Covey, he also gave us sufficient time to take our meals. He worked us hard, but always between sunrise and sunset. He required a good deal of work to be done, but gave us good tools with which to work. His farm was large, but he employed hands enough to work it, and with ease, compared with many of his neighbors. My treatment, while in his employment, was heavenly, compared with what I experienced at the hands of Mr. Edward Covey.

Mr. Freeland was himself the owner of but two slaves. Their names were Henry Harris and John Harris.[50] The rest of his hands he hired. These consisted of myself, Sandy Jenkins,* and Handy Caldwell. Henry and John were quite intelligent, and in a very little while after I went there, I succeeded in creating in them a strong desire to learn how to read. This desire soon sprang up in the others also. They very soon mustered up some old spelling-books, and nothing would do but that I must keep a Sabbath school. I agreed to do so, and accordingly devoted my Sundays to teaching these my loved fellow-slaves how to read. Neither of them knew his letters when I went

---

*This is the same man who gave me the roots to prevent my being whipped by Mr. Covey. He was "a clever soul." We used frequently to talk about the fight with Covey, and as often as we did so, he would claim my success as the result of the roots which he gave me. This superstition is very common among the more ignorant slaves. A slave seldom dies but that his death is attributed to trickery.[51]

there. Some of the slaves of the neighboring farms found what was going on, and also availed themselves of this little opportunity to learn to read. It was understood, among all who came, that there must be as little display about it as possible. It was necessary to keep our religious masters at St. Michael's unacquainted with the fact, that, instead of spending the Sabbath in wrestling, boxing, and drinking whisky, we were trying to learn how to read the will of God; for they had much rather see us engaged in those degrading sports, than to see us behaving like intellectual, moral, and accountable beings. My blood boils as I think of the bloody manner in which Messrs. Wright Fairbanks and Garrison West, both class-leaders, in connection with many others, rushed in upon us with sticks and stones, and broke up our virtuous little Sabbath school, at St. Michael's—all calling themselves Christians! humble followers of the Lord Jesus Christ! But I am again digressing.

I held my Sabbath school at the house of a free colored man, whose name I deem it imprudent to mention; for should it be known, it might embarrass him greatly, though the crime of holding the school was committed ten years ago. I had at one time over forty scholars, and those of the right sort, ardently desiring to learn. They were of all ages, though mostly men and women. I look back to those Sundays with an amount of pleasure not to be expressed. They were great days to my soul. The work of instructing my dear fellow-slaves was the sweetest engagement with which I was ever blessed. We loved each other, and to leave them at the close of the Sabbath was a severe cross indeed. When I think that these precious souls are to-day shut up in the prison-house of slavery, my feelings overcome me, and I am almost ready to ask, "Does a righteous God govern the universe? and for what does he hold the thunders in his right hand, if not to smite the oppressor, and deliver the spoiled out of the hand of the spoiler?"[52] These dear souls came not to Sabbath school because it was popular to do so, nor did I teach them because it was reputable to be thus engaged. Every moment they spent in that school, they were liable to be taken up, and given thirty-nine lashes. They came because they wished to learn. Their minds had been starved by their cruel masters. They had been shut up in mental darkness. I taught them, because it was the delight of my soul to be doing something that looked like bettering the condition of my race. I kept up my school nearly the whole year I lived with Mr. Freeland; and, beside my Sabbath school, I devoted three evenings in the week, during the winter, to teaching the slaves at home. And I have the happiness to know, that several of those who came to Sabbath school learned how to read; and that one, at least, is now free through my agency.

The year passed off smoothly. It seemed only about half as long as the year which preceded it. I went through it without receiving a single blow. I will give Mr. Freeland the credit of being the best master I ever had, *till I became my own master.* For the ease with which I passed the year, I was, however, somewhat indebted to the society of my fellow-slaves. They were noble souls; they not only possessed loving hearts, but brave ones. We were linked and interlinked with each other. I loved them with a love stronger than any thing I have experienced since. It is sometimes said that we slaves do not love and confide in each other. In answer to this assertion, I can say, I never loved any or confided in any people more than my fellow-slaves, and especially those with whom I lived at Mr. Freeland's. I believe we would have died for each other. We never undertook to do any thing, of any importance, without a mutual consultation. We never moved separately. We were one; and as much so by our tempers and dispositions, as by the mutual hardships to which we were necessarily subjected by our condition as slaves.

At the close of the year 1834, Mr. Freeland again hired me of my master, for the year 1835. But, by this time, I began to want to live *upon free land* as well as *with Freeland;* and I was no longer content, therefore, to live with him or any other slaveholder. I began, with the commencement of the year, to prepare myself for a final struggle, which should decide my fate one way or the other. My tendency was upward. I was fast approaching manhood, and year after year had passed, and I was still a slave. These thoughts roused me—I must do something. I therefore resolved that 1835 should not pass without witnessing an attempt, on my part, to secure my liberty. But I was not willing to cherish this determination alone. My fellow-slaves were dear to me. I was anxious to have them participate with me in this, my life-giving determination. I therefore, though with great prudence, commenced early to ascertain their views and feelings in regard to their condition, and to imbue their minds with thoughts of freedom. I bent myself to devising ways and means for our escape, and meanwhile strove, on all fitting occasions, to impress them with the gross fraud and inhumanity of slavery. I went first to Henry, next to John, then to the others. I found, in them all, warm hearts and noble spirits. They were ready to hear, and ready to act when a feasible plan should be proposed. This was what I wanted. I talked to them of our want of manhood, if we submitted to our enslavement without at least one noble effort to be free. We met often, and consulted frequently, and told our hopes and fears, recounted the difficulties, real and imagined, which we should be called on to meet. At times we were almost disposed to give up, and try to content ourselves with our wretched lot; at others, we were firm and unbending in our determination to go. Whenever we suggested any plan, there was shrinking—the odds were fearful. Our path was beset with the greatest obstacles; and if we succeeded in gaining the end of it, our right to be free was yet questionable—we were yet liable to be returned to bondage. We could see no spot this side of the ocean, where we could be free. We knew nothing about Canada. Our knowledge of the north did not extend farther than New York; and to go there, and be forever harassed with the frightful liability of being returned to slavery—with the certainty of being treated tenfold worse than before—the thought was truly a horrible one, and one which it was not easy to overcome. The case sometimes stood thus: At every gate through which we were to pass, we saw a watchman—at every ferry a guard—on every bridge a sentinel—and in every wood a patrol. We were hemmed in upon every side. Here were the difficulties, real or imagined—the good to be sought, and the evil to be shunned. On the one hand, there stood slavery, a stern reality, glaring frightfully upon us,—its robes already crimsoned with the blood of millions, and even now feasting itself greedily upon our own flesh. On the other hand, away back in the dim distance, under the flickering light of the north star, behind some craggy hill or snow-covered mountain, stood a doubtful freedom—half frozen—beckoning us to come and share its hospitality. This in itself was sometimes enough to stagger us; but when we permitted ourselves to survey the road, we were frequently appalled. Upon either side we saw grim death, assuming the most horrid shapes. Now it was starvation, causing us to eat our own flesh;—now we were contending with the waves, and were drowned;—now we were overtaken, and torn to pieces by the fangs of the terrible bloodhound. We were stung by scorpions, chased by wild beasts, bitten by snakes, and finally, after having nearly reached the desired spot,— after swimming rivers, encountering wild beasts, sleeping in the woods, suffering hunger and nakedness,—we were overtaken by our pursuers, and, in our resistance, we were shot dead upon the spot! I say, this picture sometimes appalled us, and made us

rather bear those ills we had,
Than fly to others, that we knew not of.[53]

In coming to a fixed determination to run away, we did more than Patrick Henry, when he resolved upon liberty or death. With us it was a doubtful liberty at most, and almost certain death if we failed. For my part, I should prefer death to hopeless bondage.[54]

Sandy, one of our number, gave up the notion, but still encouraged us. Our company then consisted of Henry Harris, John Harris, Henry Bailey, Charles Roberts, and myself. Henry Bailey was my uncle, and belonged to my master. Charles married my aunt: he belonged to my master's father-in-law, Mr. William Hamilton.

The plan we finally concluded upon was, to get a large canoe belonging to Mr. Hamilton, and upon the Saturday night previous to Easter holidays, paddle directly up the Chesapeake Bay. On our arrival at the head of the bay, a distance of seventy or eighty miles from where we lived, it was our purpose to turn our canoe adrift, and follow the guidance of the north star till we got beyond the limits of Maryland. Our reason for taking the water route was, that we were less liable to be suspected as runaways; we hoped to be regarded as fishermen; whereas, if we should take the land route, we should be subjected to interruptions of almost every kind. Any one having a white face, and being so disposed, could stop us, and subject us to examination.

The week before our intended start, I wrote several protections, one for each of us. As well as I can remember, they were in the following words, to wit:—

This is to certify that I, the undersigned, have given the bearer, my servant, full liberty to go to Baltimore, and spend the Easter holidays. Written with mine own hand, &c., 1835.

William Hamilton

Near St. Michael's, in Talbot county, Maryland

We were not going to Baltimore; but, in going up the bay, we went toward Baltimore, and these protections were only intended to protect us while on the bay.

As the time drew near for our departure, our anxiety became more and more intense. It was truly a matter of life and death with us. The strength of our determination was about to be fully tested. At this time, I was very active in explaining every difficulty, removing every doubt, dispelling every fear, and inspiring all with the firmness indispensable to success in our undertaking; assuring them that half was gained the instant we made the move; we had talked long enough; we were now ready to move; if not now, we never should be; and if we did not intend to move now, we had as well fold our arms, sit down, and acknowledge ourselves fit only to be slaves. This, none of us were prepared to acknowledge. Every man stood firm; and at our last meeting, we pledged ourselves afresh, in the most solemn manner, that, at the time appointed, we would certainly start in pursuit of freedom. This was in the middle of the week, at the end of which we were to be off. We went, as usual, to our several fields of labor, but with bosoms highly agitated with thoughts of our truly hazardous undertaking. We tried to conceal our feelings as much as possible; and I think we succeeded very well.

After a painful waiting, the Saturday morning, whose night was to witness our departure, came. I hailed it with joy, bring what of sadness it might. Friday night was a sleepless one for me. I probably felt more anxious than the rest, because I was, by common consent, at the head of the whole affair. The responsibility of success or failure lay heavily upon me. The glory of the one, and the confusion of the other, were alike mine.[55] The first two hours of that morning were such as I never experienced before, and hope never to again. Early in the morning, we went, as usual, to the field. We were spreading manure: and all at once, while thus engaged, I was overwhelmed with an indescribable feeling, in the fulness of which I turned to Sandy, who was near by, and said, "We are betrayed!" "Well," said he, "that thought has this moment struck me." We said no more. I was never more certain of any thing.

The horn was blown as usual, and we went up from the field to the house for breakfast. I went for the form, more than for want of any thing to eat that morning. Just as I got to the house, in looking out at the lane gate, I saw four white men, with two colored men. The white men were on horseback, and the colored ones were walking behind, as if tied. I watched them a few moments till they got up to our lane gate. Here they halted, and tied the colored men to the gate-post. I was not yet certain as to what the matter was. In a few moments, in rode Mr. Hamilton, with a speed betokening great excitement. He came to the door, and inquired if Master William was in. He was told he was at the barn. Mr. Hamilton, without dismounting, rode up to the barn with extraordinary speed. In a few moments, he and Mr. Freeland returned to the house. By this time, the three constables rode up, and in great haste dismounted, tied their horses, and met Master William and Mr. Hamilton returning from the barn; and after talking awhile, they all walked up to the kitchen door. There was no one in the kitchen but myself and John. Henry and Sandy were up at the barn. Mr. Freeland put his head in at the door, and called me by name, saying, there were some gentlemen at the door who wished to see me. I stepped to the door, and inquired what they wanted. They at once seized me, and, without giving me any satisfaction, tied me—lashing my hands closely together. I insisted upon knowing what the matter was. They at length said, that they had learned I had been in a "scrape," and that I was to be examined before my master; and if their information proved false, I should not be hurt.

In a few moments, they succeeded in tying John. They then turned to Henry, who had by this time returned, and commanded him to cross his hands. "I won't!" said Henry, in a firm tone, indicating his readiness to meet the consequences of his refusal. "Won't you?" said Tom Graham, the constable. "No. I won't!" said Henry, in a still stronger tone. With this, two of the constables pulled out their shining pistols, and swore, by their Creator, that they would make him cross his hands or kill him. Each cocked his pistol, and, with fingers on the trigger, walked up to Henry, saying, at the same time, if he did not cross his hands, they would blow his damned heart out. "Shoot me! shoot me!" said Henry; "you can't kill me but once. Shoot, shoot,—and be damned! *I won't be tied!*" This he said in a tone of loud defiance; and at the same time, with a motion as quick as lightning, he with one single stroke dashed the pistols from the hand of each constable. As he did this, all hands fell upon him, and, after beating him some time, they finally overpowered him, and got him tied.

During the scuffle, I managed, I know not how, to get my pass out, and, without being discovered, put it into the fire. We were all now tied; and just as we were to leave for Easton jail, Betsy Freeland, mother of William Freeland, came to the door with her hands full of biscuits, and divided them between Henry and John. She then delivered herself of a speech, to the following effect:—addressing herself to me, she said, *"You devil! You yellow devil!* it was you that put it into the heads of Henry and John to run away. But for you, you long-legged mulatto devil! Henry nor John would never have thought of such a thing."* I made no reply, and was immediately hurried off towards St. Michael's. Just a moment previous to the scuffle with Henry, Mr. Hamilton suggested the propriety of making a search for the protections which he had understood Frederick had written for himself and the rest. But, just at the moment he was about carrying his proposal into effect, his aid was needed in helping to tie Henry; and the excitement attending the scuffle caused them either to forget, or to deem it unsafe, under the circumstances, to search. So we were not yet convicted of the intention to run away.

When we got about half way to St. Michael's, while the constables having us in charge were looking ahead, Henry inquired of me what he should do with his pass. I told him to eat it with his biscuit, and own nothing; and we passed the word around, *"Own nothing;"* and *"Own nothing!"* said we all. Our confidence in each other was unshaken. We were resolved to succeed or fail together, after the calamity had befallen us as much as before. We were now prepared for any thing. We were to be dragged that morning fifteen miles behind horses, and then to be placed in the Easton jail. When we reached St. Michael's, we underwent a sort of examination. We all denied that we ever intended to run away. We did this more to bring out the evidence against us, than from any hope of getting clear of being sold; for, as I have said, we were ready for that. The fact was, we cared but little where we went, so we went together. Our greatest concern was about separation. We dreaded that more than any thing this side of death. We found the evidence against us to be the testimony of one person; our master would not tell who it was; but we came to a unanimous decision among ourselves as to who their informant was. We were sent off to the jail at Easton. When we got there, we were delivered up to the sheriff, Mr. Joseph Graham, and by him placed in jail. Henry, John, and myself, were placed in one room to-gether—Charles, and Henry Bailey, in another. Their object in separating us was to hinder concert.

We had been in jail scarcely twenty minutes, when a swarm of slave traders, and agents for slave traders, flocked into jail to look at us, and to ascertain if we were for sale. Such a set of beings I never saw before! I felt myself surrounded by so many fiends from perdition. A band of pirates never looked more like their father, the devil. They laughed and grinned over us, saying, "Ah, my boys! we have got you, haven't we." And after taunting us in various ways, they one by one went into an examination of us, with intent to ascertain our value. They would impudently ask us if we would not like to have them for our masters. We would make them no answer, and leave them to find out as best they could. Then they would curse and swear at us, telling us that they could take the devil out of us in a very little while, if we were only in their hands.

While in jail, we found ourselves in much more comfortable quarters than we expected when we went there. We did not get much to eat, nor that which was very good; but we had a good clean room, from the windows of which we could see what was going on in the street, which was very much better than though we had been placed in one of the dark, damp cells. Upon the whole, we got along very well, so far as the jail and its keeper were concerned. Immediately after the holidays were over, contrary to all our expectations, Mr. Hamilton and Mr. Freeland came up to Easton, and took Charles, the two Henrys, and John, out of jail, and carried them home, leaving me alone. I regarded this separation as a final one. It caused me more pain than any thing else in the whole transaction. I was ready for any thing rather than separation. I supposed that they had consulted together, and had decided that, as I was the whole cause of the intention of the others to run away, it was hard to make the innocent suffer with the guilty; and that they had, therefore, concluded to take the others home, and sell me, as a warning to the others that remained. It is due to the noble Henry to say, he seemed almost as reluctant at leaving the prison as at leaving home to come to the prison. But we knew we should, in all probability, be separated, if we were sold; and since he was in their hands, he concluded to go peaceably home.

I was now left to my fate. I was all alone, and within the walls of a stone prison. But a few days before, and I was full of hope. I expected to have been safe in a land of freedom; but now I was covered with gloom, sunk down to the utmost despair. I thought the possibility of freedom was gone. I was kept in this way about one week, at the end of which, Captain Auld, my master, to my surprise and utter astonishment, came up, and took me out, with the intention of sending me, with a gentleman of his acquaintance, into Alabama. But, from some cause or other, he did not send me to Alabama, but concluded to send me back to Baltimore, to live again with his brother Hugh, and to learn a trade.[56]

Thus, after an absence of three years and one month, I was once more permitted to return to my old home at Baltimore. My master sent me away, because there existed against me a very great prejudice in the community, and he feared I might be killed.

In a few weeks after I went to Baltimore, Master Hugh hired me to Mr. William Gardner, an extensive ship-builder, on Fell's Point.[57] I was put there to learn how to calk. It, however, proved a very unfavorable place for the accomplishment of this object. Mr. Gardner was engaged that spring in building two large man-of-war brigs, professedly for the Mexican government. The vessels were to be launched in the July of that year, and in failure thereof, Mr. Gardner was to lose a considerable sum; so that when I entered, all was hurry. There was no time to learn any thing. Every man had to do that which he knew how to do. In entering the ship-yard, my orders from Mr. Gardner were, to do whatever the carpenters commanded me to do. This was placing me at the beck and call of about seventy-five men. I was to regard all these as masters. Their word was to be my law. My situation was a most trying one. At times I needed a dozen pair of hands. I was called a dozen ways in the space of a single minute. Three or four voices would strike my ear at the same moment. It was—"Fred., come help me to cant this timber here."—"Fred., come carry this timber yonder."—"Fred., bring that roller here."—"Fred., go get a fresh can of water."—"Fred., come help saw off the end of this timber."—"Fred., go quick, and get the crowbar."—"Fred., hold on the end of this fall."—"Fred., go to the blacksmith's shop, and get a new punch."—"Hurra, Fred.! run and bring me a cold chisel."—"I say, Fred., bear a hand, and get up a fire as quick as lightning under that steam-box."—"Halloo, nigger! come, turn this grindstone."—"Come, come! move, move! and *bowse* this timber forward."[58]—"I say, darky, blast your eyes, why don't you heat up some pitch?"—"Halloo! halloo! halloo! (Three voices at the same time.) "Come here!—Go there!—Hold on where you are! Damn you, if you move, I'll knock your brains out!"

This was my school for eight months; and I might have remained there longer, but for a most horrid fight I had with four of the white apprentices, in which my left eye was nearly knocked out, and I was horribly mangled in other respects. The facts in the case were these: Until a very little while after I went there, white and black ship-carpenters worked side by side, and no one seemed to see any impropriety in it. All hands seemed to be very well satisfied. Many of the black carpenters were freemen. Things seemed to be going on very well. All at once, the white carpenters knocked off, and said they would not work with free colored workmen. Their reason for this, as alleged, was, that if free colored carpenters were encouraged, they would soon take the trade into their own hands, and poor white men would be thrown out of employment. They therefore felt called upon at once to put a stop to it. And, taking advantage of Mr. Gardner's necessities, they broke off, swearing they would work no longer, unless he would discharge his black carpenters. Now, though this did not extend to me in form, it did reach me in fact. My fellow-apprentices very soon began to feel it degrading to them to work with me. They began to put on airs, and talk about the "niggers" taking the country, saying we all ought to be killed; and, being encouraged by the journeymen, they commenced making my condition as hard as they could, by hectoring me around, and sometimes striking me. I, of course, kept the vow I made after the fight with Mr. Covey, and struck back again, regardless of consequences; and while I kept them from combining, I succeeded very well; for I could whip the whole of them, taking them separately. They, however, at length combined, and came upon me, armed with sticks, stones, and heavy handspikes. One came in front with a half brick. There was one at each side of me, and one behind me. While I was attending to those in front, and on either side, the one behind ran up with the handspike, and struck me a heavy blow upon the head. It stunned me. I fell, and with this they all ran upon me, and fell to beating me with their fists. I let them lay on for a while, gathering strength. In an instant, I gave a sudden surge, and rose to my hands and knees. Just as I did that, one of their number gave me, with his heavy boot, a powerful kick in the left eye. My eyeball seemed to have burst. When they saw my eye closed, and badly swollen, they left me. With this I seized the handspike, and for a time pursued them. But here the carpenters interfered, and I thought I might as well give it up. It was impossible to stand my hand against so many. All this took place in sight of not less than fifty white ship-carpenters, and not one interposed a friendly word; but some cried, "Kill the damned nigger! Kill him! kill him! He struck a white person." I found my only chance for life was in flight. I succeeded in getting away without an additional blow, and barely so; for to strike a white man is death by Lynch law,—and that was the law in Mr. Gardner's ship-yard; nor is there much of any other out of Mr. Gardner's ship-yard.

I went directly home, and told the story of my wrongs to Master Hugh; and I am happy to say of him, irreligious as he was, his conduct was heavenly, compared with that of his brother Thomas under similar circumstances. He listened attentively to my narration of the circumstances leading to the savage outrage, and gave many proofs of his strong indignation at it. The heart of my once overkind mistress was again melted into pity. My puffed-out eye and blood-covered face moved her to tears. She took a chair by me, washed the blood from my face, and, with a mother's tenderness, bound up my head, covering the wounded eye with a lean piece of fresh beef. It was almost compensation for my suffering to witness, once more, a manifestation of kindness from this, my once affectionate old mistress. Master Hugh was very much enraged. He gave expression to his feelings by pouring out curses upon the heads of those who did the deed. As soon as I got a little the better of my bruises, he took me with him to Esquire Watson's, on Bond Street, to see what could be done about the matter. Mr. Watson inquired who saw the assault committed. Master Hugh told him it was done in Mr. Gardner's ship-yard, at midday, where there were a large company of men at work. "As to that," he said, "the deed was done, and there was no question as to who did it." His answer was, he could do nothing in the case, unless some white man would come forward and testify. He could issue no warrant on my word. If I had been killed in the presence of a thousand colored people, their testimony combined would have been insufficient to have arrested one of the murderers. Master Hugh, for once, was compelled to say this state of things was too bad. Of course, it was impossible to get any white man to volunteer his testimony in my behalf, and against the white young men. Even those who may have sympathized with me were not prepared to do this. It required a degree of courage unknown to them to do so; for just at that time, the slightest manifestation of humanity toward a colored person was denounced as abolitionism, and that name subjected its bearer to frightful liabilities. The watchwords of the bloody-minded in that region, and in those days, were, "Damn the abolitionists!" and "Damn the niggers!" There was nothing done, and probably nothing would have been done if I had been killed. Such was, and such remains, the state of things in the Christian city of Baltimore.

Master Hugh, finding he could get no redress, refused to let me go back again to Mr. Gardner. He kept me himself, and his wife dressed my wound till I was again restored to health. He then took me into the ship-yard of which he was foreman, in the employment of Mr. Walter Price. There I was immediately set to calking, and very soon learned the art of using my mallet and irons. In the course of one year from the time I left Mr. Gardner's, I was able to command the highest wages given to the most experienced calkers. I was now of some importance to my master. I was bringing him from six to seven dollars per week. I sometimes brought him nine dollars per week: my wages were a dollar and a half a day. After learning how to calk, I sought my own employment, made my own contracts, and collected the money which I earned. My pathway became much more smooth than before; my condition was now much more comfortable. When I could get no calking to do, I did nothing. During these leisure times, those old notions about freedom would steal over me again. When in Mr. Gardner's employment, I was kept in such a perpetual whirl of excitement, I could think of nothing, scarcely, but my life; and in thinking of my life, I almost forgot my liberty. I have observed this in my experience of slavery,—that whenever my condition was improved, instead of its increasing my contentment, it only increased my desire to be free, and set me to thinking of plans to gain my freedom. I have found that, to make a contented slave, it is necessary to make a thoughtless one. It is necessary to darken his moral and mental vision, and, as far as possible, to annihilate the power of reason. He must be able to detect no inconsistencies in slavery; he must be made to feel that slavery is right; and he can be brought to that only when he ceases to be a man.

I was now getting, as I have said, one dollar and fifty cents per day. I contracted for it; I earned it; it was paid to me; it was rightfully my own; yet, upon each returning Saturday night, I was compelled to deliver every cent of that money to Master Hugh. And why? Not because he earned it,—not because he had any hand in earning it,—not because I owed it to him,—not because he possessed the slightest shadow of a right to it; but solely because he had the power to compel me to give it up. The right of the grim-visaged pirate upon the high seas is exactly the same.

CHAPTER XI

I now come to that part of my life during which I planned, and finally succeeded in making, my escape from slavery. But before narrating any of the peculiar circumstances, I deem it proper to make known my intention not to state all the facts connected with the transaction. My reasons for pursuing this course may be understood from the following: First, were I to give a minute statement of all the facts, it is not only possible, but quite probable, that others would thereby be involved in the most embarrassing difficulties. Secondly, such a statement would most undoubtedly induce greater vigilance on the part of slaveholders than has existed heretofore among them; which would, of course be the means of guarding a door whereby some dear brother bondman might escape his galling chains. I deeply regret the necessity that impels me to suppress any thing of importance connected with my experience in slavery. It would afford me great pleasure indeed, as well as materially add to the interest of my narrative, were I at liberty to gratify a curiosity, which I know exists in the minds of many, by an accurate statement of all the facts pertaining to my most fortunate escape. But I must deprive myself of this pleasure, and the curious of the gratification which such a statement would afford. I would allow myself to suffer under the greatest imputations which evil-minded men might suggest, rather than exculpate myself, and thereby run the hazard of closing the slightest avenue by which a brother slave might clear himself of the chains and fetters of slavery.

I have never approved of the very public manner in which some of our western friends have conducted what they call the *underground railroad*, but which, I think, by their open declarations, has been made most emphatically the *upper-ground railroad*. I honor those good men and women for their noble daring, and applaud them for willingly subjecting themselves to bloody persecution, by openly avowing their participation in the escape of slaves. I, however, can see very little good resulting from such a course, either to themselves or the slaves escaping; while, upon the other hand, I see and feel assured that those open declarations are a positive evil to the slaves remaining, who are seeking to escape. They do nothing towards enlightening the slave, whilst they do much towards enlightening the master. They stimulate him to greater watchfulness, and enhance his power to capture his slave. We owe something to the slaves south of the line as well as to those north of it; and in aiding the latter on their way to freedom, we should be careful to do nothing which would be likely to hinder the former from escaping from slavery. I would keep the merciless slaveholder profoundly ignorant of the means of flight adopted by the slave. I would leave him to imagine himself surrounded by myriads of invisible tormentors, ever ready to snatch from his infernal grasp his trembling prey. Let him be left to feel his way in the dark; let darkness commensurate with his crime hover over him; and let him feel that at every step he takes, in pursuit of the flying bondman, he is running the frightful risk of having his hot brains dashed out by an invisible agency. Let us render the tyrant no aid; let us not hold the light by which he can trace the footprints of our flying brother.[59] But enough of this. I will now proceed to the statement of those facts, connected with my escape, for which I am alone responsible, and for which no one can be made to suffer but myself.

In the early part of the year 1838, I became quite restless. I could see no reason why I should, at the end of each week, pour the reward of my toil into the purse of my master. When I carried to him my weekly wages, he would, after counting the money, look me in the face with a robber-like fierceness, and ask, "Is this all?" He was satisfied with nothing less than the last cent. He would, however, when I made him six dollars, sometimes give me six cents, to encourage me. It had the opposite effect. I regarded it as a sort of admission of my right to the whole. The fact that he gave me any part of my wages was proof, to my mind, that he believed me entitled to the whole of them. I always felt worse for having received any thing; for I feared that the giving me a few cents would ease his conscience, and make him feel himself to be a pretty honorable sort of robber. My discontent grew upon me. I was ever on the look-out for means of escape; and, finding no direct means, I determined to try to hire my time, with a view of getting money with which to make my escape. In the spring of 1838, when Master Thomas came to

Baltimore to purchase his spring goods, I got an opportunity, and applied to him to allow me to hire my time. He unhesitatingly refused my request, and told me this was another stratagem by which to escape. He told me I could go nowhere but that he could get me; and that, in the event of my running away, he should spare no pains in his efforts to catch me. He exhorted me to content myself, and be obedient. He told me, if I would be happy, I must lay out no plans for the future. He said, if I behaved myself properly, he would take care of me. Indeed, he advised me to complete thoughtlessness of the future, and taught me to depend solely upon him for happiness. He seemed to see fully the pressing necessity of setting aside my intellectual nature, in order to contentment in slavery. But in spite of him, and even in spite of myself, I continued to think, and to think about the injustice of my enslavement, and the means of escape.

About two months after this, I applied to Master Hugh for the privilege of hiring my time. He was not acquainted with the fact that I had applied to Master Thomas, and had been refused. He too, at first, seemed disposed to refuse; but, after some reflection, he granted me the privilege, and proposed the following term: I was to be allowed all my time, make all contracts with those for whom I worked, and find my own employment; and, in return for this liberty, I was to pay him three dollars at the end of each week; find myself in calking tools, and in board and clothing. My board was two dollars and a half per week. This, with the wear and tear of clothing and calking tools, made my regular expenses about six dollars per week. This amount I was compelled to make up, or relinquish the privilege of hiring my time. Rain or shine, work or no work, at the end of each week the money must be forthcoming, or I must give up my privilege. This arrangement, it will be perceived, was decidedly in my master's favor. It relieved him of all need of looking after me. His money was sure. He received all the benefits of slaveholding without its evils; while I endured all the evils of a slave, and suffered all the care and anxiety of a freeman. I found it a hard bargain. But, hard as it was, I thought it better than the old mode of getting along. It was a step towards freedom to be allowed to bear the responsibilities of a freeman, and I was determined to hold on upon it. I bent myself to the work of making money. I was ready to work at night as well as day, and by the most untiring perseverance and industry, I made enough to meet my expenses, and lay up a little money every week. I went on thus from May till August. Master Hugh then refused to allow me to hire my time longer. The ground for his refusal was a failure on my part, one Saturday night, to pay him for my week's time. This failure was occasioned by my attending a camp meeting about ten miles from Baltimore. During the week, I had entered into an engagement with a number of young friends to start from Baltimore to the camp ground early Saturday evening; and being detained by my employer, I was unable to get down to Master Hugh's without disappointing the company. I knew that Master Hugh was in no special need of the money that night. I therefore decided to go to camp meeting, and upon my return pay him the three dollars. I staid at the camp meeting one day longer than I intended when I left. But as soon as I returned, I called upon him to pay him what he considered his due. I found him very angry; he could scarce restrain his wrath. He said he had a great mind to give me a severe whipping. He wished to know how I dared go out of the city without asking his permission. I told him I hired my time, and while I paid him the price which he asked for it, I did not know that I was bound to ask him when and where I should go. This reply troubled him; and, after reflecting a few moments, he turned to me, and said I should hire my time no longer; that the next thing he should know of, I would be running away. Upon the same plea, he told me to bring my tools and clothing home forthwith. I did so; but instead of seeking work, as I had been accustomed to do previously to hiring my time, I spent the whole week without the performance of a single stroke of work. I did this in retaliation. Saturday night, he called upon me as usual for my week's wages. I told him I had no wages; I had done no work that week. Here we were upon the point of coming to blows. He raved, and swore his determination to get hold of me. I did not allow myself a single word; but was resolved, if he laid the weight of his hand upon me, it should be blow for blow. He did not strike me, but told me that he would find me in constant employment in future. I thought the matter over during the next day, Sunday, and finally resolved upon the third day of September, as the day upon which I would make a second attempt to secure my freedom. I now had three weeks during which to prepare for my journey. Early on Monday morning, before Master Hugh had time to make any engagement for me, I went out and got employment of Mr. Butler, at his ship-yard near the drawbridge, upon what is called the City Block, thus making it unnecessary for him to seek employment for me. At the end of the week, I brought him between eight and nine dollars. He seemed very well pleased, and asked me why I did not do the same the week before. He little knew what my plans were. My object in working steadily was to remove any suspicion he might entertain of my intent to run away; and in this I succeeded admirably. I suppose he thought I was never better satisfied with my condition than at the very time during which I was planning my escape. The second week passed, and again I carried him my full wages; and so well pleased was he, that he gave me twenty-five cents, (quite a large sum for a slaveholder to give a slave,) and bade me to make a good use of it. I told him I would.

Things went on without very smoothly indeed, but within there was trouble. It is impossible for me to describe my feelings as the time of my contemplated start drew near. I had a number of warm-hearted friends in Baltimore,—friends that I loved almost as I did my life,—and the thought of being separated from them forever was painful beyond expression. It is my opinion that thousands would escape from slavery, who now remain, but for the strong cords of affection that bind them to their friends. The thought of leaving my friends was decidedly the most painful thought with which I had to contend. The love of them was my tender point, and shook my decision more than all things else. Besides the pain of separation, the dread and apprehension of a failure exceeded what I had experienced at my first attempt. The appalling defeat I then sustained returned to torment me. I felt assured that, if I failed in this attempt, my case would be a hopeless one—it would seal my fate as a slave forever. I could not hope to get off with any thing less than the severest punishment, and being placed beyond the means of escape. It required no very vivid imagination to depict the most frightful scenes through which I should have to pass, in case I failed. The wretchedness of slavery, and the blessedness of freedom, were perpetually before me. It was life and death with me. But I remained firm, and, according to my resolution, on the third day of September, 1838, I left my chains, and succeeded in reaching New York without the slightest interruption of any kind. How I did so,—what means I adopted,—what direction I travelled, and by what mode of conveyance,—I must leave unexplained, for the reasons before mentioned.[60]

I have been frequently asked how I felt when I found myself in a free State. I have never been able to answer the question with any satisfaction to myself. It was a moment of the highest excitement I ever experienced. I suppose I felt as one may imagine the unarmed mariner to feel when he is rescued by a friendly man-of-war from the pursuit of a pirate. In writing to a dear friend, immediately after my arrival at New York, I said I felt like one who had escaped a den of hungry lions. This state of mind, however, very soon subsided; and I was again seized with a feeling of great insecurity and loneliness. I was yet liable to be taken back, and subjected to all the tortures of slavery. This in itself was enough to damp the ardor of my enthusiasm. But the loneliness overcame me. There I was in the midst of thousands, and yet a perfect stranger; without home and without friends, in the midst of thousands of my own brethren—children of a common Father, and yet I dared not to unfold to any one of them my sad condition. I was afraid to speak to any one for fear of speaking to the wrong one, and thereby falling into the hands of money-loving kidnappers, whose business it was to lie in wait for the panting fugitive, as the ferocious beasts of the forest lie in wait for their prey. The motto which I adopted when I started from slavery was this—"Trust no man!" I saw in every white man an enemy, and in almost every colored man cause for distrust. It was a most painful situation; and, to understand it, one must needs experience it, or imagine himself in similar circumstances. Let him be a fugitive slave in a strange land—a land given up to be the hunting-ground for slaveholders—whose inhabitants are legalized kidnappers—where he is every moment subjected to the terrible liability of being seized upon by his fellowmen, as the hideous crocodile seizes upon his prey!—I say, let him place himself in my situation—without home or friends—without money or credit—wanting shelter, and no one to give it—wanting bread, and no money to buy it,—and at the same time let him feel that he is pursued by merciless men-hunters, and in total darkness as to what to do, where to go, or where to stay,—perfectly helpless both as to the means of defence and means of escape,—in the midst of plenty, yet suffering the terrible gnawings of hunger,—in the midst of houses, yet having no home,—among fellow-men, yet feeling as if in the midst of wild beasts, whose greediness to swallow up the trembling and half-famished fugitive is only equalled by that with which the monsters of the deep swallow up the helpless fish upon which they subsist,—I say, let him be placed in this most trying situation,—the situation in which I was placed,— then, and not till then, will he fully appreciate the hardships of, and know how to sympathize with, the toil-worn and whip-scarred fugitive slave.[61]

Thank Heaven, I remained but a short time in this distressed situation. I was relieved from it by the humane hand of Mr. David Ruggles, whose vigilance, kindness, and perseverance, I shall never forget.[62] I am glad of an opportunity to express, as far as words can, the love and gratitude I bear him. Mr. Ruggles is now afflicted with blindness, and is himself in need of the same kind offices which he was once so forward in the performance of toward others. I had been in New York but a few days, when Mr. Ruggles sought me out, and very kindly took me to his boarding-house at the corner of Church and Lespenard Streets. Mr. Ruggles was then very deeply engaged in the memorable *Darg* case, as well as attending to a number of other fugitive slaves, devising ways and means for their successful escape; and, though watched and hemmed in on almost every side, he seemed to be more than a match for his enemies.

Very soon after I went to Mr. Ruggles, he wished to know of me where I wanted to go; as he deemed it unsafe for me to remain in New York. I told him I was a calker, and should like to go where I could get work. I thought of going to Canada; but he decided against it, and in favor of my going to New Bedford, thinking I should be able to get work there at my trade. At this time, Anna,* my intended wife, came on; for I wrote to her immediately after my arrival at New York, (notwithstanding my homeless, houseless, and

*She was free.

Anna Murray Douglass, wife of Frederick Douglass

helpless condition,) informing her of my successful flight, and wishing her to come on forthwith.[63] In a few days after her arrival, Mr. Ruggles called in the Rev. J. W. C. Pennington, who, in the presence of Mr. Ruggles, Mrs. Michaels, and two or three others, performed the marriage ceremony, and gave us a certificate, of which the following is an exact copy:—

This may certify, that I joined together in holy matrimony Frederick Johnson* and Anna Murray, as man and wife, in the presence of Mr. David Ruggles and Mrs. Michaels.

James W. C. Pennington[64]

New York, Sept. 15, 1838

Upon receiving this certificate, and a five-dollar bill from Mr. Ruggles, I shouldered one part of our baggage, and Anna took up the other, and we set out forthwith to take passage on board of the steamboat John W. Richmond

*I had changed my name from Frederick *Bailey* to that of *Johnson*.

for Newport, on our way to New Bedford. Mr. Ruggles gave me a letter to a Mr. Shaw in Newport, and told me, in case my money did not serve me to New Bedford, to stop in Newport and obtain further assistance; but upon our arrival at Newport, we were so anxious to get to a place of safety, that, notwithstanding we lacked the necessary money to pay our fare, we decided to take seats in the stage, and promise to pay when we got to New Bedford. We were encouraged to do this by two excellent gentlemen, residents of New Bedford, whose names I afterward ascertained to be Joseph Ricketson and William C. Taber. They seemed at once to understand our circumstances, and gave us such assurance of their friendliness as put us fully at ease in their presence. It was good indeed to meet with such friends, at such a time. Upon reaching New Bedford, we were directed to the house of Mr. Nathan Johnson, by whom we were kindly received, and hospitably provided for. Both Mr. and Mrs. Johnson took a deep and lively interest in our welfare. They proved themselves quite worthy of the name of abolitionists. When the stage-driver found us unable to pay our fare, he held on upon our baggage as security for the debt. I had but to mention the fact to Mr. Johnson, and he forthwith advanced the money.

We now began to feel a degree of safety, and to prepare ourselves for the duties and responsibilities of a life of freedom. On the morning after our arrival at New Bedford, while at the breakfast-table, the question arose as to what name I should be called by. The name given me by my mother was, "Frederick Augustus Washington Bailey." I, however, had dispensed with the two middle names long before I left Maryland so that I was generally known by the name of "Frederick Bailey." I started from Baltimore bearing the name of "Stanley." When I got to New York, I again changed my name to "Frederick Johnson," and thought that would be the last change. But when I got to New Bedford, I found it necessary again to change my name. The reason of this necessity was, that there were so many Johnsons in New Bedford, it was already quite difficult to distinguish between them. I gave Mr. Johnson the privilege of choosing me a name, but told him he must not take from me the name of "Frederick." I must hold on to that, to preserve a sense of my identity. Mr. Johnson had just been reading the "Lady of the Lake," and at once suggested that my name be "Douglass." From that time until now I have been called "Frederick Douglass;" and as I am more widely known by that name than by either of the others, I shall continue to use it as my own.[65]

I was quite disappointed at the general appearance of things in New Bedford. The impression which I had received respecting the character and condition of the people of the north, I found to be singularly erroneous. I had very strangely supposed, while in slavery, that few of the comforts, and scarcely any of the luxuries, of life were enjoyed at the north, compared with what were enjoyed by the slaveholders of the south. I probably came to this conclusion from the fact that northern people owned no slaves. I supposed that they were about upon a level with the non-slaveholding population of the south. I knew *they* were exceedingly poor, and I had been accustomed to regard their poverty as the necessary consequence of their being non-slaveholders. I had somehow imbibed the opinion that, in the absence of slaves, there could be no wealth, and very little refinement. And upon coming to the north, I expected to meet with a rough, hard-handed, and uncultivated population, living in the most Spartan-like simplicity, knowing nothing of the ease, luxury, pomp, and grandeur of southern slaveholders. Such being my conjectures, any one acquainted with the appearance of New Bedford may very readily infer how palpably I must have seen my mistake.

In the afternoon of the day when I reached New Bedford, I visited the wharves, to take a view of the shipping. Here I found myself surrounded with the strongest proofs of wealth. Lying at the wharves, and riding in the stream, I saw many ships of the finest model, in the best order, and of the largest size. Upon the right and left, I was walled in by granite warehouses of the widest dimensions, stowed to their utmost capacity with the necessaries and comforts of life. Added to this, almost every body seemed to be at work, but noiselessly so, compared with what I had been accustomed to in Baltimore. There were no loud songs heard from those engaged in loading and unloading ships. I heard no deep oaths or horrid curses on the laborer. I saw no whipping of men; but all seemed to go smoothly on. Every man appeared to understand his work, and went at it with a sober, yet cheerful earnestness, which betokened the deep interest which he felt in what he was doing, as well as a sense of his own dignity as a man. To me this looked exceedingly strange. From the wharves I strolled around and over the town, gazing with wonder and admiration at the splendid churches, beautiful dwellings, and finely-cultivated gardens; evincing an amount of wealth, comfort, taste, and refinement, such as I had never seen in any part of slaveholding Maryland.[66]

Every thing looked clean, new and beautiful. I saw few or no dilapidated houses, with poverty-stricken inmates; no half-naked children and bare-footed women, such as I had been accustomed to see in Hillsborough, Easton, St. Michael's, and Baltimore. The people looked more able, stronger, healthier, and happier, than those of Maryland. I was for once made glad by a view of extreme wealth, without being saddened by seeing extreme poverty. But the most astonishing as well as the most interesting thing to me was the condition of the colored people, a great many of whom, like myself, had escaped thither as a refuge from the hunters of men. I found many, who had not been seven years out of their chains, living in finer houses, and evidently enjoying more of the comforts of life, than the average of slaveholders in Maryland. I will venture to assert that my friend Mr. Nathan Johnson (of whom I can say with a grateful heart, "I was hungry, and he gave me meat; I was thirsty, and he gave me drink; I was a stranger, and he took me in")[67] lived in a neater house; dined at a better table; took, paid for, and read, more newspapers; better understood the moral, religious, and political character of the nation,—than nine tenths of the slaveholders in Talbot county, Maryland. Yet Mr. Johnson was a working man. His hands were hardened by toil, and not his alone, but those also of Mrs. Johnson.[68] I found the colored people much more spirited than I had supposed they would be. I found among them a determination to protect each other from the blood-thirsty kidnapper, at all hazards. Soon after my arrival, I was told of a circumstance which illustrated their spirit. A colored man and a fugitive slave were on unfriendly terms. The former was heard to threaten the latter with informing his master of his whereabouts. Straightway a meeting was called among the colored people, under the stereotyped notice, "Business of importance!" The betrayer was invited to attend. The people came at the appointed hour, and organized the meeting by appointing a very religious old gentleman as president, who, I believe, made a prayer, after which he addressed the meeting as follows: *"Friends, we have got him here, and I would recommend that you young men just take him outside the door, and kill him!"* With this, a number of them bolted at him; but they were intercepted by some more timid than themselves, and the betrayer escaped their vengeance, and has not been seen in New Bedford since. I believe there have been no more such threats, and should there be hereafter, I doubt not that death would be the consequence.

I found employment, the third day after my arrival, in stowing a sloop with a load of oil. It was new, dirty, and hard work for me; but I went at it with a glad heart and a willing hand. I was now my own master. It was a happy moment, the rapture of which can be understood only by those who have been slaves. It was the first work, the reward of which was to be entirely my own. There was no Master Hugh standing ready, the moment I earned the money, to rob me of it. I worked that day with a pleasure I had never before experienced. I was at work for myself and newly-married wife. It was to me the starting-point of a new existence. When I got through with that job, I went in pursuit of a job of calking; but such was the strength of prejudice against color, among the white calkers, that they refused to work with me, and of course I could get no employment.* Finding my trade of no

*I am told that colored persons can now get employment at calking in New Bedford—a result of anti-slavery effort.

immediate benefit, I threw off my calking habiliments, and prepared myself to do any kind of work I could get to do. Mr. Johnson kindly let me have his wood-horse and saw, and I very soon found myself a plenty of work. There was no work too hard—none too dirty. I was ready to saw wood, shovel coal, carry the hod, sweep the chimney, or roll oil casks,—all of which I did for nearly three years in New Bedford, before I became known to the antislavery world.

In about four months after I went to New Bedford, there came a young man to me, and inquired if I did not wish to take the "Liberator."[69] I told him I did; but, just having made my escape from slavery, I remarked that I was unable to pay for it then. I, however, finally became a subscriber to it. The paper came, and I read it from week to week with such feelings as it would be quite idle for me to attempt to describe. The paper became my meat and my drink. My soul was set all on fire. Its sympathy for my brethren in bonds—its scathing denunciations of slaveholders—its faithful exposures of slavery—and its powerful attacks upon the upholders of the institution— sent a thrill of joy through my soul, such as I had never felt before!

I had not long been a reader of the "Liberator," before I got a pretty correct idea of the principles, measures and spirit of the anti-slavery reform. I took right hold of the cause. I could do but little; but what I could, I did with a joyful heart, and never felt happier than when in an anti-slavery meeting. I seldom had much to say at the meetings, because what I wanted to say was said so much better by others. But, while attending an anti-slavery convention at Nantucket, on the 11th of August, 1841, I felt strongly moved to speak, and was at the same time much urged to do so by Mr. William C. Coffin, a gentleman who had heard me speak in the colored people's meeting at New Bedford. It was a severe cross, and I took it up reluctantly. The truth was, I felt myself a slave, and the idea of speaking to white people weighed me down. I spoke but a few moments, when I felt a degree of freedom, and said what I desired with considerable ease. From that time until now, I have been engaged in pleading the cause of my brethren—with what success, and with what devotion, I leave those acquainted with my labors to decide.

APPENDIX

I find, since reading over the foregoing Narrative that I have, in several instances, spoken in such a tone and manner, respecting religion, as may possibly lead those unacquainted with my religious views to suppose me an opponent of all religion. To remove the liability of such misapprehension, I deem it proper to append the following brief explanation. What I have said respecting and against religion, I mean strictly to apply to the *slaveholding religion* of this land, and with no possible reference to Christianity proper; for, between the Christianity of this land, and the Christianity of Christ, I recognize the widest possible difference—so wide, that to receive the one as good, pure, and holy, is of necessity to reject the other as bad, corrupt, and wicked. To be the friend of the one, is of necessity to be the enemy of the other. I love the pure, peaceable, and impartial Christianity of Christ: I therefore hate the corrupt, slaveholding, women-whipping, cradle-plundering, partial and hypocritical Christianity of this land. Indeed, I can see no reason, but the most deceitful one, for calling the religion of this land Christianity. I look upon it as the climax of all misnomers, the boldest of all frauds, and the grossest of all libels. Never was there a clearer case of "stealing the livery of the court of heaven to serve the devil in." I am filled with unutterable loathing when I contemplate the religious pomp and show, together with the horrible inconsistencies, which every where surround me. We have men-stealers for ministers, women-whippers for missionaries, and cradle-plunderers for church members. The man who wields the blood-clotted cowskin during the week fills the pulpit on Sunday, and claims to be a minister of the meek and lowly Jesus. The man who robs me of my earnings at the end of each week meets me as a class-leader on Sunday morning, to show me the way of life, and the path of salvation. He who sells my sister, for purposes of prostitution, stands forth as the pious advocate of purity. He who proclaims it a religious duty to read the Bible denies me the right of learning to read the name of the God who made me. He who is the religious advocate of marriage robs whole millions of its sacred influence, and leaves them to the ravages of wholesale pollution. The warm defender of the sacredness of the family relation is the same that scatters whole families,—sundering husbands and wives, parents and children, sisters and brothers,—leaving the hut vacant, and the hearth desolate. We see the thief preaching against theft, and the adulterer against adultery. We have men sold to build churches, women sold to support the gospel, and babes sold to purchase Bibles for the *poor heathen! all for the glory of God and the good of souls!* The slave auctioneer's bell and the church-going bell chime in with each other, and the bitter cries of the heart-broken slave are drowned in the religious shouts of his pious master. Revivals of religion and revivals in the slave-trade go hand in hand together. The slave prison and the church stand near each other. The clanking of fetters and the rattling of chains in the prison, and the pious psalm and solemn prayer in the church, may be heard at the same time. The dealers in the bodies and souls of men erect their stand in the presence of the pulpit, and they mutually help each other. The dealer gives his blood-stained gold to support the pulpit, and the pulpit, in return, covers his infernal business with the garb of Christianity. Here we have religion and robbery the allies of each other—devils dressed in angels' robes, and hell presenting the semblance of paradise.[70]

> Just God! and these are they,
>   Who minister at thine altar, God of right!
> Men who their hands, with prayer and blessing, lay
>   On Israel's ark of light.
>
> What! preach, and kidnap men?
>   Give thanks, and rob thy own afflicted poor?
> Talk of thy glorious liberty, and then
>   Bolt hard the captive's door?
>
> What! servants of thy own
>   Merciful Son, who came to seek and save
> The homeless and the outcast, fettering down
>   The tasked and plundered slave!
>
> Pilate and Herod friends!
>   Chief priests and rulers, as of old, combine!
> Just God and holy! is that church which lends
>   Strength to the spoiler thine?[71]

The Christianity of America is a Christianity, of whose votaries it may be as truly said, as it was of the ancient scribes and Pharisees, "They bind heavy burdens, and grievous to be borne, and lay them on men's shoulders, but they themselves will not move them with one of their fingers. All their works they do for to be seen of men.——They love the uppermost rooms at feasts, and the chief seats in the synagogues, ... and to be called of men, Rabbi, Rabbi.——But woe unto you, scribes and Pharisees, hypocrites! for ye shut up the kingdom of heaven against men; for ye neither go in yourselves, neither suffer ye them that are entering to go in. Ye devour widows' houses, and for a pretence make long prayers; therefore ye shall receive the greater damnation. Ye compass sea and land to make one prose-lyte, and when he is made, ye make him twofold more the child of hell than yourselves.——Woe unto you, scribes and Pharisees, hypocrites! for ye pay tithe of mint, and anise, and cumin, and have omitted the weightier matters of the law, judgment, mercy, and faith; these ought ye to have done, and not to leave the other undone. Ye blind guides! which strain at a gnat, and swallow a camel. Woe unto you, scribes and Pharisees, hypocrites! for ye make clean the outside of the cup and of the platter; but within, they are full of extortion and excess.——Woe unto you, scribes and Pharisees, hypo-crites! for ye are like unto whited sepulchres, which indeed appear beautiful outward, but are within full of dead men's bones, and of all uncleanness.

Even so ye also outwardly appear righteous unto men, but within ye are full of hypocrisy and iniquity."[72]

Dark and terrible as is this picture, I hold it to be strictly true of the overwhelming mass of professed Christians in America. They strain at a gnat, and swallow a camel. Could any thing be more true of our churches? They would be shocked at the proposition of fellowshipping a *sheep*-stealer; and at the same time they hug to their communion a *man*-stealer, and brand me with being an infidel, if I find fault with them for it. They attend with Pharisaical strictness to the outward forms of religion, and at the same time neglect the weightier matters of the law, judgment, mercy, and faith. They are always ready to sacrifice, but seldom to show mercy. They are they who are represented as professing to love God whom they have not seen, whilst they hate their brother whom they have seen. They love the heathen on the other side of the globe. They can pray for him, pay money to have the Bible put into his hand, and missionaries to instruct him; while they despise and totally neglect the heathen at their own doors.

Such is, very briefly, my view of the religion of this land; and to avoid any misunderstanding, growing out of the use of general terms, I mean, by the religion of this land, that which is revealed in the words, deeds, and actions, of those bodies, north and south, calling themselves Christian churches, and yet in union with slaveholders. It is against religion, as presented by these bodies, that I have felt it my duty to testify.

I conclude these remarks by copying the following portrait of the religion of the south, (which is, by communion and fellowship, the religion of the north,) which I soberly affirm is "true to the life," and without caricature or the slightest exaggeration. It is said to have been drawn, several years before the present anti-slavery agitation began, by a northern Methodist preacher, who, while residing at the south, had an opportunity to see slaveholding morals, manners, and piety, with his own eyes. "Shall I not visit for these things? saith the Lord. Shall not my soul be avenged on such a nation as this?"[73]

A PARODY

Come, saints and sinners, hear me tell
How pious priests whip Jack and Nell,
And women buy and children sell,
And preach all sinners down to hell,
    And sing of heavenly union.

They'll bleat and baa, [go on] like goats,
Gorge down black sheep, and strain at motes,
Array their backs in fine black coats,

Then seize their negroes by their throats,
And choke, for heavenly union.

They'll church you if you sip a dram,
And damn you if you steal a lamb;
Yet rob old Tony, Doll, and Sam,
Of human rights, and bread and ham;
     Kidnapper's heavenly union.

They'll loudly talk of Christ's reward,
And bind his image with a cord,
And scold, and swing the lash abhorred,
And sell their brother in the Lord
     To handcuffed heavenly union.

They'll read and sing a sacred song,
And make a prayer both loud and long,
And teach the right and do the wrong,
Hailing the brother, sister throng,
     With words of heavenly union.

We wonder how such saints can sing,
Or praise the Lord upon the wing,
Who roar, and scold, and whip, and sting,
And to their slaves and mammon cling,
     In guilty conscience union.

They'll raise tobacco, corn, and rye,
And drive, and thieve, and cheat, and lie,
And lay up treasures in the sky,
By making switch and cowskin fly,
     In hope of heavenly union.

They'll crack old Tony on the skull,
And preach and roar like Bashan bull,
Or braying ass, of mischief full,
Then seize old Jacob by the wool,
     And pull for heavenly union.

A roaring, ranting, sleek man-thief,
Who lived on mutton, veal, and beef,
Yet never would afford relief
To needy, sable sons of grief,
     Was big with heavenly union.

"Love not the world," the preacher said,
And winked his eye, and shook his head;
He seized on Tom, and Dick, and Ned,
Cut short their meat, and clothes, and bread,
     Yet still loved heavenly union.

Another preacher whining spoke
Of One whose heart for sinners broke:
He tied old Nanny to an oak,
And drew the blood at every stroke,
    And prayed for heavenly union.

Two others oped their iron jaws,
And waved their children-stealing paws;
There sat their children in gewgaws;
By stinting negroes' backs and maws,
    They kept up heavenly union.

All good from Jack another takes,
And entertains their flirts and rakes,
Who dress as sleek as glossy snakes,
And cram their mouths with sweetened cakes;
    And this goes down for union.[74]

Sincerely and earnestly hoping that this little book may do something toward throwing light on the American slave system, and hastening the glad day of deliverance to the millions of my brethren in bonds—faithfully relying upon the power of truth, love, and justice, for success in my humble efforts—and solemnly pledging myself anew to the sacred cause,—I subscribe myself,

Frederick Douglass

Lynn, Mass., April 28, 1845

THE END

NOTES ON THE TEXT

Preface and Letter

[1]Garrison's biblical references are Psalms 8:5; Hebrews 2:7, 9.

[2]This physical description of Douglass at his first abolitionist speech demonstrates not only the fugitive slave's compelling image but also the ways in which Garrison and his colleagues would use him as an exhibit ("ornament") for antislavery audiences.

[3]In this paragraph Garrison gives a conventional guarantee of authenticity, common in slave narratives prefaced by white abolitionists. "SLAVERY AS IT IS" may refer to Theodore Weld, *American Slavery As It Is: Testimony of a Thousand Witnesses* (New York, 1839; rpt. New York: Arno Press, 1968), a best-selling compilation of southern newspaper accounts of brutalities toward slaves published the year after Douglass's escape.

[4]William Lloyd Garrison (1805–79), editor of *The Liberator,* published in Boston, radical abolitionist and social reformer, principal founder of the Massachusetts and American Anti-Slavery societies. The ending of the preface indicates how Garrison turned this document into a typical exhortatory abolitionist speech; at the same time it is a celebration of Douglass's extraordinary abilities.

[5]Wendell Phillips (1811–84), born and raised in Boston's merchant class. Phillips became a leading abolitionist orator, social reformer, and later labor advocate. He was a close friend of Douglass during the 1840s.

[6]Both Phillips and Garrison make special mention of the passage about the "white sails" on the Chesapeake and stress, as Douglass does so often in the text, that slavery bound mind and soul as well as body.

[7]Phillips's conclusion is a standard argument for the Garrisonian doctrine of "disunion."

Narrative

[1]Considerable evidence indicates that Douglass was born in February 1818; he was, therefore, twenty-seven years old while writing the *Narrative.* The question of his age and birth date plagued Douglass throughout his life. For the most conclusive scholarly work on his birth date, see Dickson J. Preston, *Young Frederick Douglass: The Maryland Years* (Baltimore: Johns Hopkins University Press, 1980), 31–34. Preston's work has been a tremendous aid in preparing these notes; it is the best and most detailed source on Douglass's family background and his years as a slave.

[2]Harriet Bailey (1792–1825), Douglass's mother, the second of twelve children born to Betsey and Isaac Bailey, in whose cabin he was born and lived the first five and one-half years of his life. Frederick was one of seven children born to Harriet between 1813 and 1825. In this autobiography Douglass has very little recall of his mother, but in *My Bondage and My Freedom* (1855), 52–54, his image of her changes markedly. Ten years after the *Narrative,* his mother had become the object of "scanty, but very distinct" memory, and of deep yearning. "Her personal appearance and bearing are ineffaceably stamped upon my memory. She was tall, and finely proportioned; of deep black, glossy complexion; had regular features, and, among the other slaves, was remarkably sedate in her manners." Douglass even found a picture in James Pritchard's *Natural History of Man* (London, 1848) that reminded him of his mother. According to Pritchard, the picture is actually a likeness of the Egyptian pharaoh Rameses. Hence the reference is full of irony, since the picture is not only that of a man but that of a figure who does not have obvious African features. Betsey Bailey (1774–1849) lived a relatively independent slave existence and had a strong influence on Frederick's early years. Isaac Bailey was a free black who worked as a wood sawyer. Douglass was part of the fifth generation, born in America, of the Bailey family.

[3]Three times in the first chapter Douglass writes either that his master was his father or that his father was a white man. Douglass's treatment of the identity of his father through his three autobiographies is intriguing. From the first to the third text, his father diminishes from the white man about whom Douglass speculates in the *Narrative* to a man merely "shrouded in mystery" in *My Bondage and My Freedom* to this stark statement in *Life and Times* (1881): "Of my father I know nothing." Circumstantial evidence points, though not conclusively, to either Aaron Anthony or Thomas Auld as Douglass's father. See Preston, *Young Frederick Douglass,* 23; William S. McFeely, *Frederick Douglass* (New York: W. W. Norton, 1991), 13, 40–43.

[4]The story of Ham and the curse of Noah is from Genesis 9:20–27. Douglass here confronts the widespread phenomenon of mixed race (mulatto) children born during slavery.

[5]Aaron Anthony (1767–1826), a Lloyd plantation overseer. Douglass knew him during 1824–26.

[6]Edward Lloyd V (1779–1834), governor of Maryland, U.S. senator, and owner of vast plantations. Under his ownership, the Lloyd holdings included 550 slaves; by the eve of the Civil War, his son Edward Lloyd VI owned 700 slaves in Maryland, Louisiana, Arkansas, and Mississippi. Aunt Hester is Hester Bailey, the eighth child of Betsey, born 1810.

[7]"My master" refers to Aaron Anthony. Thomas Auld (1795–1880) grew up near St. Mich-

aels, Maryland, and was trained as a seaman. He was for a time captain of Colonel Lloyd's sloop, *Sally Lloyd.* He later becomes Douglass's owner.

⁸On the Wye plantation itself in 1824, the year Douglass arrived, there were 181 slaves. Preston, *Young Frederick Douglass,* 48.

⁹Austin Woolfolk, a notorious Baltimore slave trader. In 1828, his firm's best profit year, he netted approximately $28,000. In the first fourteen years of Douglass's life, one sister, two aunts, seven first cousins, and at least five other relatives, as well as a number of other slaves he knew well, were "sold South," many of them by Woolfolk. Preston, *Young Frederick Douglass,* 76.

¹⁰Actually William Sevier, overseer of the central farm of the Lloyd plantation. He had responsibility for approximately 165 slaves.

¹¹James Hopkins, overseer.

¹²This passage illustrates the Garrisonian doctrine of antipartyism, but this ironic play on representative democracy also shows Douglass's sense of the slaves' abilities to make the most of their daily lives and of the political and moral economy of slavery.

¹³Quotation from "The Time-Piece," book 2, line 8, in William Cowper, *The Task* (1785).

¹⁴Douglass's estimate of Lloyd's holdings in slaves is high. The Book of Job had special meanings for Douglass. He claimed that in his first memory of hearing Sophia Auld read to him aloud as a slave boy, lying under a table, her text was the first chapter of Job. See *The Liberator,* 27 Feb. 1846. His reference here may be Job 1:3.

¹⁵Here Douglass portrays a structure of virtual totalitarianism in the master-slave relationship, similar to that offered in Stanley M. Elkins, *Slavery: A Problem in American Institutional and Intellectual Life* (Chicago: University of Chicago Press, 1959).

¹⁶Jepson was actually Jacob Gibson, who was not nearly as wealthy as Colonel Lloyd. Here Douglass suggests a world of reciprocity and paternalism in the master-slave relationship similar to that portrayed in Eugene D. Genovese, *Roll, Jordan, Roll: The World the Slaves Made* (New York: Random House, 1974).

¹⁷Douglass inaccurately remembered the first name of Orson Gore, overseer.

¹⁸Bill Denby. Douglass uses both spellings. Lloyd plantation records indicate that Denby died in 1823, lending some credence to this story of Gore's alleged killing of the slave. See Preston, *Young Frederick Douglass,* 72–73.

¹⁹The correct name is Thomas Lambdin, a ship's carpenter.

²⁰No record has been found of this murder, nor of the warrant for the woman's arrest. But a Mr. Giles Hicks did live in Caroline County, Maryland, which is where Anna Murray grew up. Preston, *Young Frederick Douglass,* 74.

²¹The correct name is John Beale Bordley, Jr. The portrayal of these murders illustrates Douglass's use of his autobiography to write a stinging polemic against all the worst evils of slavery, such as these crimes committed in a lawless environment. *My Bondage and My Freedom,* ten years later, was a much more introspective work, muting somewhat these public-polemical features.

²²Note the two senses of time in this passage: then and now, past and present. This metaphor of the pen in the gashes caused by shoelessness in the cold is one of Douglass's uses of indirection to stress the meaning of literacy to a slave. On this notion of two senses of time, see Albert E. Stone, "Identity and Art in Frederick Douglass; Narrative," *CLA Journal* 17 (1973), 192–213.

²³An image perhaps of baptismal, ritual cleansing, foreshadowing freedom in that new, mysterious place called Baltimore.

²⁴Sophia Auld, wife of Hugh Auld. She is Douglass's "Miss Sopha" in both *My Bondage and My Freedom,* 142, and *Life and Times,* 76. Douglass first learned to read with Sophia Auld, and he frequently told this tender part of his story on the abolitionist platform, using Sophia as both a potential mother symbol and an example of slavery's denial of such attachments.

²⁵The biblical reference for "ministering angels" is probably Matthew 4:11. Douglass's discussion of divine providence, faith, and a sense of chosenness reflects his religious outlook during these years. Douglass elaborates more on his youthful religious conversion in *My Bondage and My Freedom,* 166–69.

²⁶Hugh Auld (1799–1861), younger brother of Thomas. He owned a shipbuilding business in

Baltimore. Neither Hugh nor Thomas Auld ever made any serious effort to capture Douglass once he had escaped from slavery. Douglass's freedom was purchased for him by British antislavery friends. In December 1846, Hugh Auld received $711.66 for Douglass, and the bill of sale was filed in the Baltimore Chattel Records Office. Preston, *Young Frederick Douglass,* 175.

[27]In this text Douglass tells us very little about the free black community of Baltimore, which was one of the largest concentrations of free people of color in the South. By 1850 Baltimore had approximately 7,000 slaves, 175,000 whites, and nearly 30,000 free blacks. Anna Murray, Douglass's future wife, was one of those free blacks.

[28]Caleb Bingham, *The Columbian Orator: Containing a Variety of Original and Selected Pieces Together With Rules calculated to Improve Youth and Others in the Ornamental and Useful Art of Eloquence* (Boston: Manning and Loring, 1797). Douglass bought a secondhand copy of this book for fifty cents at Nathaniel Knight's bookstore on Thames Street in Baltimore. It contains a remarkable collection of speeches from classical times and from the Age of Revolution by Cato, Socrates, Napoleon, George Washington, William Pitt the elder, Charles James Fox, and others. In these speeches, as well as in the crucial "Dialogue between a Master and Slave," Douglass encountered passage after passage about freedom, liberty, democracy, courage, virtue, and so forth. He especially learned and recited passages about the multilayered antithesis of slavery and bondage. Bingham's book also included a guide to techniques of oratory and eloquence. The future great orator and prophet of freedom could not have found a more useful and meaningful book at this point in his youth.

[29]Instead of Sheridan, Douglass actually refers here to Daniel O'Connor's "Speech in the Irish House of Commons, in Favour of the Bill for Emancipating the Roman Catholics, 1795."

[30]This memorable passage about the dual nature of literacy—its curse as well as its blessing—is part of a tradition in African American autobiography. For another classic example, see *The Autobiography of Malcolm X,* with the assistance of Alex Haley (New York: Grove Press, 1964), 172–73.

[31]Douglass was thirteen years old during Nat Turner's rebellion in August 1831. It may have been at that time that he first read about "abolitionists" in the *Baltimore American.* See Preston, *Young Frederick Douglass,* 100–101.

[32]Petitions had been a major tool of the antislavery movement in the North since the late eighteenth century. The practice was revived with great energy in the 1830s. By 1835 the volume of abolitionist petitions flooding Congress reached such a level of controversy that the infamous "gag rule" was engineered to prevent their open discussion. By 1838, the year Douglass escaped from slavery, the American Anti-Slavery Society claimed that a total of 415,000 petitions had been sent to Washington, D.C. See James B. Stewart, *Holy Warriors: The Abolitionists and American Slavery* (New York: Hill and Wang, 1976), 81–84.

[33]Master Andrew and the variety of other overseers in this book may have served as models for Harriet Beecher Stowe in her creation of the character Simon Legree in *Uncle Tom's Cabin* (1852).

[34]Douglass erred in this accusation against Thomas Auld regarding the treatment of his grandmother. After Isaac Bailey died, Betsey Bailey was actually taken in by Auld's own household. Auld saw to it that Betsey, going blind, was cared for until she died in November 1849. In Douglass's famous public letter to Auld in 1848, he makes no retraction of the story. But in a letter published in the *North Star,* 7 Sept. 1849, Douglass apologized and admitted to being "unjust and unkind." He also admitted the mistake in his famous reunion with Auld on the Eastern Shore, as the latter was dying in June 1877. See Preston, *Young Frederick Douglass,* 186.

[35]John Greenleaf Whittier, "The Farewell" (1835), in *Poems of John Greenleaf Whittier* (Boston: Ticknor and Fields, 1857), 163.

[36]The biblical reference is Jeremiah 5:29. This passage is striking for its fictional qualities; not only is it based on inaccuracies, which may not matter in this sense, but Douglass leaves the first person altogether and imagines the scene of his grandmother's demise in sentimental terms.

[37]Eliza Mitchell (b. March 1816, d. after 1870), Douglass's sister; Priscilla Bailey (b. 1816), Douglass's aunt; Henny (b. September 1816, d. after 1840), Douglass's cousin. Preston, *Young Frederick Douglass,* 206.

[38]The biblical reference is Luke 12:47.

[39]Edward Covey (1806–75), a now famous character in slave narrative literature, was a real person. He rented a 150-acre farm in Talbot County, Maryland, when Douglass was sent to him; in 1836 he purchased a farm of 196 acres.

[40]Actually January 1834. Douglass was sixteen years old.

[41]This passage is possibly influenced by Psalm 137 in which during the Babylonian captivity, the children of Israel are asked while "carried . . . away captive" to "sing the Lord's song in a strange land." In his Fourth of July speech in 1852, Douglass quotes from Psalm 137 at length. See "The Meaning of July Fourth for the Negro," Rochester, New York, July 5, 1852, in Philip S. Foner, ed., *The Life and Writings of Frederick Douglass,* vol. 2 (New York: International Publishers, 1950), 189.

[42]Here Douglass may be drawing upon the great lament in the Book of Job. The reference may be either Job 7:11 or Job 10:1.

[43]This famous passage is at once a Job-like lament about Douglass's "dark night of slavery," a psalmlike prayer of deliverance written almost in a teenager's voice, and a cry of assurance based on the Negro spiritual "Better Days Are Coming."

[44]Bill Smith, a slave of about thirty years old, who had been hired from his owner, Samuel Harrison; William Hughes, Covey's cousin; and Eli, another hired slave. Preston, *Young Frederick Douglass,* 119, 123.

[45]Sandy Jenkins, property of William Groome, an Easton, Maryland, merchant, married to a free woman with her own cabin. He was hired out to Mrs. Covey's father, Mr. Caulk. Preston, *Young Frederick Douglass,* 125, 227.

[46]It is unlikely that Covey was actually a professional slave breaker on his small farm, an idea that has become an article of faith in some Douglass literature and one that Douglass himself promoted. Covey had "hired" young Frederick from Auld. Covey did not go on to suffer a disgraceful fate, as would be the case in sentimental literature. He became a prosperous farmer; at his death in 1875, his estate was worth $15,559. Preston, *Young Frederick Douglass,* 129.

[47]This section on holidays and drinking is a standard abolitionist-temperance message of the time. At this moment, the polemical character of the writing prevents Douglass from finding the subtlety or reciprocity in the "cunning" of the master-slave relationship.

[48]William Freeland, owned a farm along the Miles River, approximately three miles from St. Michaels, Maryland.

[49]Rev. Daniel Weeden, Methodist minister; Rev. Rigby Hopkins, Methodist Episcopal minister. There is supporting evidence for Douglass's claims against Weeden. In 1839 Weeden forced Samuel Brooks, a free black man, back into slavery, then bought him. Preston, *Young Frederick Douglass,* 227.

[50]Henry and John Harris, brothers, slaves of William Freeland. On Douglass's close relationship to the Harrises, see McFeely, *Frederick Douglass,* 49–55.

[51]Sandy Jenkins's root, and Douglass's footnote about "superstition" refer, if indirectly, to survivals of African beliefs in the spirit world.

[52]This is likely a paraphrase, combining Exodus 15:6–17 and Isaiah 33:1.

[53]Shakespeare's *Hamlet,* act 3, sc. 1, lines 81–82.

[54]For readers accustomed to stories of the Underground Railroad, Douglass's bravado and imagination here would have been very effective. In this section he creates a vision of a fearful but self-made Underground Railroad. The reference to Patrick Henry is to the Virginian's "Give me liberty or give me death" speech in Richmond in 1775. Here Douglass seeks to set himself and his followers apart from Henry ("we did more"); at the same time he stakes out a place in the American Revolutionary tradition. He may also be responding to Garrison's use of Patrick Henry in the preface.

[55]Here Douglass keeps himself at the center of the narrative, a prime example of the manner in which he was creating the image of the self-made hero. Many scholars have discussed the

similarity of this aspect of Douglass's autobiographies to Benjamin Franklin's classic *Autobiography* (1790), and even to the Horatio Alger stories. See Rafia Zafar, "Franklinian Douglass: The Afro-American as Representative Man," in Eric J. Sundquist, ed., *Frederick Douglass: New Literary and Historical Essays* (Cambridge: Cambridge University Press, 1990), 99–117; Peter F. Walker, *Moral Choices: Memory, Desire, and Imagination in Nineteenth Century American Abolition* (Baton Rouge: Louisiana State University Press, 1978), 213–16; and Waldo E. Martin, *The Mind of Frederick Douglass* (Chapel Hill: University of North Carolina Press, 1984), 254–56.

[56]Thomas Auld's decision to send Frederick back to Baltimore was a turning point in Douglass's life. On the significance of this decision, see McFeely, *Frederick Douglass*, 56–57.

[57]William Gardner, owner of a large shipbuilding yard in Baltimore. An irony of Douglass's work at Gardner's is that at least four ships destined for the slave trade were built there during 1836–38, the period of his labor as a caulker. Douglass was, in all likelihood, unaware of the ultimate purpose of these ships. Preston, *Young Frederick Douglass*, 143, 228.

[58]A nautical term for the rope on a tackle or hoisting device; to "bouse" would be to haul the timbers.

[59]This appeal for secrecy in aiding fugitives is also an interesting vision into Douglass's developing thought about violence toward slaveholders. At this time he was on the surface a Garrisonian nonresistant (opposed to violence), but by the late 1840s and early 1850s he came to endorse the slaves' right to violent rebellion. This position is anticipated here as he wishes the slaveholder to be left with the "frightful risk of having his hot brains dashed out by an invisible agency." See David W. Blight, *Frederick Douglass' Civil War: Keeping Faith in Jubilee* (Baton Rouge: Louisiana State University Press, 1989), 92–100.

[60]In the later autobiographies Douglass explains many of the details of his escape. The journey is epic in its courage, logistics, and result. With the moral and financial support of Anna Murray, Douglass plotted the immediate escape for three weeks. According to family lore, Anna sold one of her feather beds to help raise money for him. Douglass obtained "seaman's protection" papers from a retired black sailor named Stanley. Disguised as a sailor on leave, dressed in a red shirt, a wide-brimmed hat, and a loosely tied black cravat (sailor style), and prepared to "talk sailor like an old salt," Douglass took the northbound train from Baltimore. A black friend and hackman, Isaac Rolles, drove Douglass to the station, where he boarded the train at the last minute, avoiding the ticket windows where, his "free papers" would surely have been scrutinized. The conductor, who handled other blacks gruffly aboard the train, had a soft spot for sailors (as did many Americans at that time) and hardly examined Douglass's papers. At Havre de Grace, Maryland, Douglass boarded a ferry to cross the Susquehanna River. Every stop brought a new tension or terror; on the ferry he encountered a black deckhand he knew well who openly wanted to know what he was doing there. Douglass ducked the questions, was otherwise undetected, and successfully crossed. He then boarded a train to Wilmington, Delaware, where he encountered two white men who knew him, a ship's captain from the Baltimore yards and a German blacksmith. The captain did not notice the twenty-year-old fugitive, and Douglass was convinced that his German acquaintance simply decided not to betray him. At Wilmington, Douglass boarded a steamboat for Philadelphia, where he paused only briefly to reflect on free soil, then inquired of a black passerby about the train to New York City. By the night train, and a final ferry across the Hudson River, Douglass arrived in New York on the morning of 4 Sept. 1838, broke and alone. After a harrowing night and another day of hiding and wandering the streets of lower Manhattan, Douglass found his way to David Ruggles, the stalwart leader of the free black Vigilance Committee. Under Ruggles's protection, Douglass wrote to his bride in Baltimore, and Anna hastily traveled safely north to join him. As Douglass reports here, they were married on 15 Sept. by James W. C. Pennington, in New York. The dreams and imaginings of freedom were beginning to come true. See *My Bondage and My Freedom*, 335–41; *Life and Times*, 187–205; McFeely, *Frederick Douglass*, 69–73.

[61]This passage demonstrates a classic aspect of abolitionist polemical literature—the terror-stricken world of the fugitive slave at risk in a sea of "pirates," "crocodiles," "men-hunters," and "wild beasts."

[62]David Ruggles, free black grocer, activist, and abolitionist, leader and founder of the New

York Vigilance Committee, the organization that helped protect and aid the escapes and lives of fugitive slaves. During its first three years of operation in the 1830s, Ruggles reported that the committee's network handled approximately one fugitive slave every other day. Douglass's experience, though heroic indeed, was not unique. See Jane H. Pease and William H. Pease, *They Who Would Be Free: Blacks' Search for Freedom, 1830–1861* (New York: Atheneum, 1974), 179–81, 207–12.

[63]Anna Murray Douglass (1813–82), the eighth of twelve children born to free parents in Caroline County, on Maryland's eastern shore. Facts about Anna's life are scarce, in part because Douglass told us so little about his wife. As a teenager and young woman in Baltimore, where Douglass met her, Anna worked as a domestic. She had a reputation as a strong-willed and meticulous housekeeper, and during forty-four years of marriage with Douglass she raised five children while the abolitionist father and husband traveled the country and the world. Anna never learned to read and write, which is another factor in the lack of information on her life. See McFeely, *Frederick Douglass*, 66–67, 218–19.

[64]James W. C. Pennington (1807–70), born a slave in Queen Annes County, Maryland, escaped from slavery in 1827. He became a blacksmith and later a Presbyterian minister, abolitionist, and author of *The Fugitive Blacksmith; or, Events in the History of James W. C. Pennington, Pastor of a Presbyterian Church in New York, Formerly a Slave in the State of Maryland, United States* (London: Charles Gilpin, 1850). See R. J. M. Blackett, *Beating against the Barriers: Biographical Essays in Nineteenth Century Afro-American History* (Baton Rouge: Louisiana State University Press, 1986), 1–84.

[65]New Bedford was a prosperous port city. Douglass's new name was taken from the heroic character Douglas (to which the fugitive added an *s*) in Sir Walter Scott's poem *Lady of the Lake* (1810), a historical romance set in the Scottish Highlands in the sixteenth century. The story is about the banishment and redemption of James of Douglas; the tale of heroic retrieval of identity and freedom was loosely comparable to Douglass's story. See *The Poetical Works of Sir Walter Scott*, vol. 3 (Philadelphia, 1839), 5–300.

[66]This contrast of the northern and southern political economies, using New Bedford, represents an evolving political antislavery position that would take on great significance in the 1850s and with the coming of the Civil War. It contrasts the work and dignity associated with free labor with the sloth and backwardness of slave labor. Such comparisons would become staple and compelling parts of the ideology of the Free-Soil and Republican parties in the 1850s.

[67]This is a direct quotation from Matthew 25:35.

[68]The Johnsons are offered as symbols of two ideas essential to the free black experience in the North: free blacks as political citizens and as self-sufficient laborers and producers.

[69]William Lloyd Garrison's weekly abolitionist newspaper, published in Boston, 1831–65. Soon Douglass's early career would be chronicled in this paper.

[70]Attacks on religious hypocrisy were a very common part of Douglass's rhetoric during his pre–Civil War years. This appendix appears as a kind of apology, but it is really much more; it is a classic of Garrisonian doctrine, a masterful use of antithesis, and a splendid illustration of Douglass's place in the jeremiadic tradition.

[71]John Greenleaf Whittier's poem "Clerical Oppressors" (1836), in *The Works of John Greenleaf Whittier*, vol. 3 (Boston: Ticknor and Fields, 1848), 38–40.

[72]Douglass paraphrases the story of the Pharisees and the scribes, derived from Matthew 23 and Luke 11:39–52.

[73]The biblical reference is Jeremiah 5:29. This demonstrates a deeply political and unconventional ending for a slave narrative. Here we see the terrible warning of a black Jeremiah in the juxtapositions of freedom and slavery, Christianity and slaveholding, in a republic.

[74]This is Douglass's parody of "Heavenly Union," a hymn sung especially in southern churches. It also represents Douglass's widely recognized oratorical ability of mimicry, especially of slaveholders and the southern clergy.

PART TWO

Selected Reviews, Documents, and Speeches

CALEB BINGHAM

Dialogue Between
a Master and a Slave

"Dialogue Between a Master and a Slave," in Caleb Bingham, The Columbian Orator: Containing a Variety of Original and Selected Pieces Together With Rules calculated to Improve Youth and Others in the Ornamental and Useful Art of Eloquence *(Boston: Manning and Loring, 1797), 240–42. Caleb Bingham (1757–1817) was a Massachusetts teacher and writer. The* Columbian Orator *became the standard manual on oratory in early-nineteenth-century America. Douglass discovered, purchased, and studied this volume while he was a youthful slave in Maryland. In the* Narrative *he makes special reference to the excerpt reprinted here. The dialogue's romantic and unlikely conclusion served as inspiration to Douglass during years when his freedom remained in the realm of imagination.*

MASTER: Now villain! what have you to say for this feigned attempt to run away? Is there any punishment that you do not deserve?

SLAVE: I well know that nothing I can say will avail. I submit to my fate.

MAST: But are you not a base fellow, a hardened and ungrateful rascal?

SLAVE: I am a slave. That is answer enough.

MAST: I am not content with that answer. I thought I discerned in you some tokens of a mind superior to your condition. I treated you accordingly. You have been comfortably fed and lodged, not over-worked, and attended with the most humane care when you were sick. And this is the return?

SLAVE: Since you condescend to talk to me, as man to man, I will reply. What have you done, what can you do for me, that will compensate for the liberty which you have taken away?

MAST: I did not take it away. You were a slave when I fairly purchased you.

SLAVE: Did I give my consent to the purchase?

MAST: You had no consent to give. You had already lost the right of disposing of yourself.

SLAVE: I had lost the power, but how the right? I was treacherously kidnapped in my own country, when following an honest occupation. I was put in chains, sold to one of your countrymen, carried by force on board his ship, brought hither, and exposed to sale like a beast in the market, where you bought me. What step in all this progress of violence and injustice can give a *right?* Was it in the villain who stole me, in the slave-merchant who tempted him to do so, or in you who encouraged the slave-merchant to bring his cargo of human cattle to cultivate your lands?

MAST: It is in the order of Providence that one man should become subservient to another. It ever has been so, and ever will be. I found the custom, and did not make it.

SLAVE: You cannot but be sensible, that the robber who puts a pistol to your breast may make just the same plea. Providence gives him a power over your life and property; it gave my enemies a power over my liberty. But it has also given me legs to escape with; and what should prevent me from using them? Nay, what should restrain me from retaliating the wrongs I have suffered, if a favorable occasion should offer?

MAST: Gratitude; I repeat gratitude! Have I not endeavored ever since I possessed you to alleviate your misfortunes by kind treatment: and does that confer no obligation? Consider how much worse your condition might have been under another master.

SLAVE: You have done nothing for me more than your working cattle. Are they not well fed and tended? do you work them harder than your slaves? is not the rule of treating both designed only for your own advantage? You treat both your men and beast slaves better than some of your neighbors, because you are more prudent and wealthy than they.

MAST: You might add, more humane too.

SLAVE: Humane! Does it deserve that appellation to keep your fellow-men in forced subjection, deprived of all exercise of their free will, liable to all the injuries that your own caprice, or the brutality of your overseers, may heap on them, and devoted, soul and body, only to your pleasure and emolument? Can gratitude take place between creatures in such a state, and the tyrant who holds them in it? Look at these limbs; are they not those of a man? Think that I have the spirit of a man too.

MAST: But it was my intention not only to make your life tolerably comfortable at present, but to provide for you in your old age.

SLAVE: Alas! is a life like mine, torn from country, friends, and all I hold dear, and compelled to toil under the burning sun for a master, worth thinking about for old age? No; the sooner it ends, the sooner I shall obtain that relief for which my soul pants.

MAST: Is it impossible, then, to hold you by any ties but those of constraint and severity?

SLAVE: It is impossible to make one, who has felt the value of freedom, acquiesce in being a slave.

Mast: Suppose I were to restore you to your liberty, would you reckon that a favor?

Slave: The greatest; for although it would only be undoing a wrong, I know too well how few among mankind are capable of sacrificing interest to justice, not to prize the exertion when it is made.

Mast: I do it, then; be free.

Slave: Now I am indeed your servant, though not your slave. And as the first return I can make for your kindness, I will tell you freely the condition in which you live. You are surrounded with implacable foes, who long for a safe opportunity to revenge upon you and the other planters all the miseries they have endured. The more generous their natures, the more indignant they feel against that cruel injustice which has dragged them hither, and doomed them to perpetual servitude. You can rely on no kindness on your parts to soften the obduracy of their resentment. You have reduced them to the state of brute beasts; and if they have not the stupidity of beasts of burden, they must have the ferocity of beasts of prey. Superior force alone can give you security. As soon as that falls, you are at the mercy of the merciless. Such is the social bond between master and slave!

MARGARET FULLER

Review of Narrative of the Life of Frederick Douglass, An American Slave

Review of Narrative of the Life of Frederick Douglass, An American Slave, *by Margaret Fuller,* New York Tribune, *June 10, 1845, reprinted from William L. Andrews, ed.,* Critical Essays on Frederick Douglass *(Boston: G. K. Hall, 1991), 21–23. This review concluded by quoting the last four paragraphs of chapter 2 of the* Narrative, *but that quotation has been deleted here. Margaret Fuller (1810–50) was a distinguished literary critic, Transcenden-*

talist, teacher, writer, and author of Woman in the Nineteenth Century *(1845) and numerous other works and translations.*

Frederick Douglass has been for some time a prominent member of the Abolition party. He is said to be an excellent speaker—can speak from a thorough personal experience—and has upon the audience, beside, the influence of a strong character and uncommon talents. In the book before us he has put into the story of his life the thoughts, the feelings, and the adventures that have been so affecting through the living voice; nor are they less so from the printed page. He has had the courage to name the persons, times and places, thus exposing himself to obvious danger, and setting the seal on his deep convictions as to the religious need of speaking the whole truth. Considered merely as a narrative, we have never read one more simple, true, coherent, and warm with genuine feeling. It is an excellent piece of writing, and on that score to be prized as a specimen of the powers of the Black Race, which Prejudice persists in disputing. We prize highly all evidence of this kind, and it is becoming more abundant. The Cross of the Legion of Honor has just been conferred in France on Dumas and Soulie, both celebrated in the paths of light and literature. Dumas, whose father was a General in the French Army, is a Mulatto; Soulie, a Quadroon. He went from New Orleans, where, though to the eye a white man, yet as known to have African blood in his veins, he could never have enjoyed the privileges due to a human being. Leaving the Land of Freedom, he found himself free to develop the powers that God had given.

Two wise and candid thinkers,—the Scotchman, Kinment, prematurely lost to this country, of which he was so faithful and generous a student, and the late Dr. Channing,—both thought that the African Race had in them a peculiar element, which, if it could be assimilated with those imported among us from Europe would give to genius a development, and to the energies of character a balance and harmony beyond what has been seen heretofore in the history of the world. Such an element is indicated in their lowest estate by a talent for melody, a ready skill at imitation and adaptation, an almost indestructible elasticity of nature. It is to be remarked in the writings both of Soulie and Dumas, full of faults but glowing with plastic life and fertile in invention. The same torrid energy and saccharine fulness may be felt in the writings of this Douglass, though his life being one of action or resistance, was less favorable to SUCH powers than one of a more joyous flow might have been.

The book is prefaced by two communications—one from Garrison and one from Wendell Phillips. That from the former is in his usual over-emphatic style. His motives and his course have been noble and generous. We look upon him with high respect, but he has indulged in violent invective and denunciation till he has spoiled the temper of his mind. Like a man who has been in the habit of screaming himself hoarse to make the deaf better, he can no longer pitch his voice on a key agreeable to common ears. Mr. Phillips's remarks are equally decided, without this exaggeration in the tone. Douglass himself seems very just and temperate. We feel that his view, even of those who have injured him most, may be relied upon. He knows how to allow for motives and influences. Upon the subject of Religion, he speaks with great force, and not more than our own sympathies can respond to. The inconsistencies of Slaveholding professors of religion cry to Heaven. We are not disposed to detest, or refuse communion with them. Their blindness is but one form of that prevalent fallacy which substitutes a creed for a faith, a ritual for a life. We have seen too much of this system of atonement not to know that those who adopt it often began with good intentions, and are, at any rate, in their mistakes worthy of the deepest pity. But that is no reason why the truth should not be uttered, trumpet-tongued, about the thing. "Bring no more vain oblations": sermons must daily be preached anew on that text. Kings, five hundred years ago, built churches with the spoils of war; Clergymen to-day command Slaves to obey a Gospel which they will not allow them to read, and call themselves Christians amid the curses of their fellow men. The world ought to get on a little faster than that, if there be really any principle of movement in it. The Kingdom of Heaven may not at the beginning have dropped seed larger than a mustard seed, but even from that we had a right to expect a fuller growth than can be believed to exist, when we read such a book as this of Douglass. Unspeakably affecting is the fact that he never saw his mother at all by day light. "I do not recollect of ever seeing my mother by the light of day. She was with me in the night. She would lie down with me, and get me to sleep, but long before I waked she was gone."

The following extract presents a suitable answer to the background argument drawn by the defender of Slavery from the songs of the Slave, and it is also a good specimen of the powers of observation and manly heart of the writer. We wish that every one may read his book and see what a mind might have been stifled in bondage—what a man may be subjected to the insults of spendthrift dandies, or the blows of mercenary brutes, in whom there is no whiteness except of the skin, no humanity except in the outward form, and of whom the Avenger will not fail yet to demand—"where is thy brother?"

EPHRAIM PEABODY

Narratives of Fugitive Slaves

"Narratives of Fugitive Slaves," by Ephraim Peabody, a review of three works: Douglass's Narrative; The Life of Josiah Henson, *Samuel A. Eliot, ed. (Boston: A. D. Phelps, 1849); and William Wells Brown,* Narrative of William W. Brown, a Fugitive Slave, Written by Himself *(Boston: American Anti-Slavery Society, 1847), in* Christian Examiner *47 (July 1849), 61–93. This excerpt is reprinted from William L. Andrews, ed.,* Critical Essays on Frederick Douglass *(Boston: G. K. Hall, 1991), 24–27. Ephraim Peabody (1807–56) was a clergyman, graduate of Bowdoin College, pastor of a Unitarian church in New Bedford, Massachusetts, 1838–46, and, for the remainder of his life, pastor of King's Chapel, Boston.*

America has the mournful honor of adding a new department to the literature of civilization,—the autobiographies of escaped slaves. . . . The subjects of two of these narratives, Frederick Douglass and Josiah Henson, we have known personally, and, apart from the internal evidence of truth which their stories afford, we have every reason to put confidence in them as men of veracity. The authors of the remaining accounts are, for anything we know to the contrary, equally trustworthy. We place these volumes without hesitation among the most remarkable productions of the age,—remarkable as being pictures of slavery by the slave, remarkable as disclosing under a new light the mixed elements of American civilization, and not less remarkable as a vivid exhibition of the force and working of the native love of freedom in the individual mind.

There are those who fear lest the elements of poetry and romance should fade out of the tame and monotonous social life of modern times. There is no danger of it while there are any slaves left to seek for freedom, and to tell the story of their efforts to obtain it. There is that in the lives of men who have sufficient force of mind and heart to enable them to struggle up from hopeless bondage to the position of freemen, beside which the ordinary characters of romance are dull and tame. They encounter a whole Iliad of woes, not in plundering and enslaving others, but in recovering for themselves those rights of which they have been deprived from birth. Or if the Iliad should be thought not to present a parallel case, we know not where one who wished to write a modern Odyssey could find a better subject than in the adventures of a fugitive slave. What a combination of qualities and deeds and sufferings most fitted to attract human sympathy in each particular case! . . .

These biographies of fugitive slaves are calculated to exert a very wide influence on public opinion. We have always been familiar with slavery, as seen from the side of the master. These narratives show how it looks as seen from the side of the slave. They contain the *victim's account* of the working of this great institution. When one escapes from the South, and finds an opportunity of speaking and has the power to speak, it is certain that he will have attentive listeners. Not only curiosity, but a sense of justice, predisposes men to hear the testimony given by those who have suffered, and who have had few among their own number to describe their sufferings. The extent of the influence such lives must exert may be judged of, when we learn the immense circulation which has been secured for them. Of Brown's Narrative, first published in 1847, not less than eight thousand copies have been already sold. Douglass's Life, first published in 1845, has in this country alone passed through seven editions, and is, we are told, now out of print. They are scattered over the whole of the North, and all theoretical arguments for or against slavery are feeble, compared with these accounts by living men of what they personally endured when under its dominion. . . .

The narrative of Douglass contains the life of a superior man. Since his escape from slavery, he has been employed as an antislavery lecturer, and is now the editor of a newspaper in Rochester, N.Y. He does not belong to the class, always small, of those who bring to light great principles, or who originate new methods of carrying them out. He has, however, the vividness of sensibility and of thought which we are accustomed to associate with a Southern climate. He has a natural and ready eloquence, a delicacy of taste, a quick perception of proprieties, a quick apprehension of ideas, and a felicity of expression, which are possessed by few among the more cultivated, and which are surprising when we consider that it is but a few years since he was a slave. In any popular assembly met for the discussion of subjects with which he has had the opportunity to become familiar, he is a man to command and hold attention. He is a natural orator, and his original endowments and the peculiarity of his position have given him a high place among antislavery speakers.

But while our sympathies go strongly with him, and because they go with him, we are disposed to make a criticism on a mode of address in which he sometimes indulges himself, which we believe is likely to diminish, not only his usefulness, but his real influence. We would not detract from his merits, and we can easily excuse in him a severity of judgment and a one-sidedness of view which might be inexcusable in another. We can hardly condemn one who has been a slave for seeing only the evils of slavery, and for thinking lightly of the difficulty of remedying them; but we have wished, when we have heard him speak, or read what he has written, that he might wholly avoid a fault from which a natural magnanimity does something towards saving him, but to which he is nevertheless exposed. His associates at the North have been among those who are apt to mistake violence and extravagance of expression and denunciation for eloquence;—men who, whatever their virtues otherwise, are not in the habit of using discrimination to their judgments of men or of measures which they do not approve. To him they have doubtless been true and faithful friends, and he naturally adopts their style of speech. But it is a mistaken one, if the speaker wishes to sway the judgment of his hearers and to accomplish any practical end. No matter what the vehemence of tone or expression, whenever a public speaker indulges himself in violent and unqualified statements and in sweeping denunciations, he not only makes it apparent that he is deficient in a sound and fair judgment, but what is worse, he creates in his hearers a secret distrust of his real earnestness,—a vague feeling that after all he is thinking more of his speech than of the end for which he professes to make it. When men are profoundly in earnest, they are not apt to be extravagant. The more earnest, the more rigidly true. A merchant, in discussing the politics of the day, about which he knows or cares little, freely indulges in loose, extravagant, and violent declarations. But follow him to his counting-room; let him be making inquiries or giving directions about some enterprise which he really has deeply at heart, and the extravagance is gone. Nothing will answer here but truth, and the exact truth. His earnestness makes him calm. It is seen in the moderated accuracy, as well as in the decision and strength, of his statements. Extravagance and passion and rhetorical flourishes might do when nothing which he greatly valued was at stake; but here is something too serious for trifling. Just so it is in other cases. A flippant, extravagant speaker, especially if he be gifted with the power of sarcasm, will probably be listened to and applauded, but nothing comes of it. They who applaud the most understand very well that this is not the kind of person whose judgment is to be relied on as a guide in action. His words are listened to with much the same sort of interest that is given to the personated passion of the theatre. A few sober words from a calm, wise, discriminating mind are, after all, the ones which are followed. Nothing is less effective, for any practical end, than the "withering and scorching" eloquence with which American speeches seem so to abound. It conciliates no opponent, and though it may light up the momentary passions, it gives no new strength of conviction to the friends of a cause. It is the last kind of eloquence to be cultivated by those who are heartily in earnest in their desire to promote any great reform.

We by no means think that these remarks apply peculiarly to Douglass. We make them, however, because we think that, more often than he is probably aware, he suffers himself to fall into this mode of speech. He has such ability to appeal to the higher and more generous sentiments, and such appeals do so much to win over enemies and to strengthen friends, he has such personal knowledge of slavery, and is so competent to make all he says effective, through candor and a just appreciation of the difficulties that beset the subject of emancipation, and is withal so much of a man, that we regret any mistake of judgment which tends to diminish his power as an advocate of the antislavery cause.

We have hesitated about making these remarks; and now, on reading them over, the sympathy which his narrative excites, and our respect for the force of character he has shown in rising from the depths of bondage to be equal associate of those who have possessed every opportunity of cultivation and refinement, almost make us erase what we have written. We would avoid giving pain to one who has suffered all that we should most dread ourselves, and who has risen above obstacles by which we should probably have been crushed. But still, whatever the past has been, he is now free. By his indisputable deserts, he has secured for himself an influential position. The course which he takes is important to others beside himself. Should he read this criticism, we hope that the internal evidence will be sufficient to show that it is written by one who rejoices in his usefulness. And in the faith that he may so read it, and that its suggestions may not be without value, we allow it to stand.

There are many passages in the narrative of Douglass which we should be pleased to quote, but it has been so long published and so widely circulated, that many of our readers have probably seen it. We would only say, in conclusion, that we feel a deep interest in his career. He is one of the living evidences that there is in the colored population of the South no natural incapacity for the enjoyment of freedom; and he occupies a position and possesses abilities which enable him, if he pursues a wise course, to be a most useful laborer in the cause of human rights.

NATHANIEL P. ROGERS
Southern Slavery
and Northern Religion:
Two Addresses

"Southern Slavery and Northern Religion," two addresses delivered in Concord, New Hampshire, February 11, 1844, as reported by Nathaniel P. Rogers, in [Concord, N.H.] Herald of Freedom, *February 16, 1844. Rogers was an abolitionist and editor of the* Herald of Freedom. *The version published here is reprinted from John W. Blassingame, ed.,* The Frederick Douglass Papers, *series 1, vol. 1 (New Haven; Yale University Press, 1979), 23–27. Shortly after giving these speeches Douglass began writing the* Narrative *at his home in Lynn, Massachusetts.*

Frederick Douglass lectured here Sunday evening, to a crowded Court House. He was here during all Sunday, and spoke at our Sunday meetings, and it was known generally to the people here, and there was great curiosity to see him, and hear his eloquence. But no meeting house was offered to him,—or to the people, rather, who wished to hear him—and would have been profoundly interested in the grandeur of his speech. He had to speak, and the audience had to hear, in an inconvenient, uncomfortable room. The sects know here, that Anti-slavery will never again ask them for a meeting house. We will furnish them orators of the first cast, and they are in famishing want of good speaking—but they must come to the cold and noisy Court Room and dirty Town Hall, to hear, so long as they shut up their clean and comfortable synagogues against us. We have asked for them long enough. It would be dishonorable begging, to ask again. If the meeting house is *capable* of being opened to the truth, they had better offer them to us. I believe it is not capable of it—and therefore that they will never open them to anti-slavery. I would here suggest that there ought to be a Lyceum Hall erected in this place, where TRUTH could be spoken. What a commentary on the character of the numerous Temples here. I tell the people the Truth *can never be admitted into an Idol Temple.*

Douglass spoke excellently Sunday afternoon, and to a pretty numerous audience—many of them not accustomed to attend our meetings.—He was advertised as a "fugitive *from* slavery." He said he was not a fugitive *from* slavery—but a fugitive *slave.* He was a fugitive, he said, not *from* slavery—but *in* slavery. To get from it—he must go beyond the limits of the American Union. He asked them why it was that he—such as they saw him before them, must wander about in their midst, a *fugitive* and a *slave.* He *demanded* the reason. It is because of your Religion, he sternly replied, which sanctifies the system under which I suffer, and dooms me to it, and the millions of my brethren now in bondage. Your religion justifies our tyrants, and you are yourselves our enslavers. I see my enslavers here in Concord, and before my eyes—if any are here who countenance the church and the religion of your country. Other influences helped sustain the system of slavery, he said, but this is its sanctioner and main support.

In the evening Douglass made a masterly and most impressive speech. The house was crowded, and with the best of our people—no clergy—and but few of the bigots, who are past hearing. He began by a calm, deliberate and very simple narrative of his life. He did not detail personal sufferings—though he said he might—if inclined to. His fate had been mild compared to that of slaves generally. He, to be sure, had to go naked, pretty much during the earlier years of childhood, and feed at a trough like a pig, under the care of his old grandmother, who, past her labor, was turned out, charged to dig her own subsistence, and that of a few little ones, out of a patch of ground allotted her. These little ones were separated from their mothers, that they might early be without ties of kindred. He did not remember his mother, I think he said, and never knew who was his father. He never knew in his first six years anything about a bed—any more than the pigs did. He remembered stealing an old salt bag, into which he used to creep, and sleep, on the earth floor of the negro hut, at his old grandmother's. She, by the way, had reared twelve children of her own, for the market—all sold and gone from her—and she now blind and alone, if she is alive, and none left with her to bring her a cup of cold water. His own back he said was scarred with the whip—but still he had been a favored slave. He was sent to a slave-breaker, when some 16 or 17 years old—his master not being able to manage him. An attempt at breaking him once brought on a struggle between him and the Jockey. The result of it was such that the Jockey did not care to repeat it, while his care for his reputation, as a successful breaker, kept him from getting help to manage a slave boy—and Frederick escaped farther whipping from him afterwards.—After narrating his early life briefly—his *schooling*—the beginning of the wife of his master's relative to teach him letters, and the stern forbidding of it, by her husband—which Frederick overheard—how he caught a little teaching here and there from the children in the streets—a fact, he said, which accounted to him for his extraordinary attachment to children—after getting through this, in a somewhat suppressed and hesitating way—interesting all the while for its facts, but dullish in manner—and giving I suspect, no token to the audience of what was coming—though I discerned, at times, symptoms of a brewing storm—he closed his slave narrative, and gradually let out the outraged humanity that was laboring in him, in indignant and terrible speech. It was not what you could describe as oratory or eloquence. It was sterner—darker—deeper than these. It was the volcanic outbreak of human nature long pent up in slavery and at last bursting its imprisonment. It was the storm of insurrection—and I could not but think, as he stalked to and fro on the platform, roused up like the Numidian Lion—how that terrible voice of his would ring through the pine glades of the South, in the day of her visitation—calling the insurgents to battle and striking terror to the hearts of the dismayed and despairing mastery. He reminded me of Toussaint among the plantations of Haiti.—There was great oratory in his speech—but more of dignity and earnestness than what we call eloquence. He was not up as a speaker—performing. He was an insurgent slave taking hold on the right of speech, and charging on his tyrants the bondage of his race. One of our Editors ventured to cross his path by a rash remark. He better have run upon a Lion. It was fearful, but magnificent, to see how magnanimously and lion-like the royal fellow tore him to pieces, and left his untouched fragments scattered around him.

FREDERICK DOUGLASS

My Slave Experience in Maryland

"My Slave Experience in Maryland," an address delivered in New York City, May 6, 1845, as recorded in National Antislavery Standard, *May 22, 1845. The version published here is reprinted from John W. Blassingame, ed.,* The Frederick Douglass Papers, *series 1, vol. 1, (New Haven: Yale University*

Press, 1979), 27–34. Douglass had completed the Narrative *approximately one week before this speech, and it is believed to be the first time he divulged specific facts of his slave background.*

Frederick Douglas[s] was next introduced to the audience, Mr. Garrison observing that he was one who, by the laws of the South, had been *a chattel* but who was now, by his own intrepid spirit and the laws of God, *a man.* He proceeded:—I do not know that I can say anything to the point. My habits and early life have done much to unfit me for public speaking, and I fear that your patience has already been wearied by the lengthened re- marks of other speakers, more eloquent than I can possibly be, and better prepared to command the attention of the audience. And I can scarcely hope to get your attention even for a longer period than fifteen minutes.

Before coming to this meeting, I had a sort of desire—I don't know but it was vanity—to stand before a New-York audience in the Tabernacle. But when I came in this morning, and looked at those massive pillars, and saw the vast throng which had assembled, I got a little frightened, and was afraid that I could not speak; but now that the audience is not so large and I have recovered from my fright, I will venture to say a word on Slavery.

I ran away from the South seven years ago—passing through this city in no little hurry, I assure you—and lived about three years in New Bedford, Massachusetts, before I became publicly known to the anti-slavery people. Since then I have been engaged for three years in telling the people what I know of it. I have come to this meeting to throw in my mite, and since no fugitive slave has preceded me, I am encouraged to say a word about the sunny South. I thought, when the eloquent female who addressed this audi- ence a while ago, was speaking of the horrors of Slavery, that many an honest man would doubt the truth of the picture which she drew; and I can unite with the gentleman from Kentucky in saying, that she came far short of describing them.

I can tell you what I have seen with my own eyes, felt on my own person, and know to have occurred in my own neighborhood. I am not from any of those States where the slaves are said to be in their most degraded condition; but from Maryland, where Slavery is said to exist in its mildest form; yet I can stand here and relate atrocities which would make your blood to boil at the statement of them. I lived on the plantation of Col. Lloyd, on the eastern shore of Maryland, and belonged to that gentleman's clerk. He owned, probably, not less than a thousand slaves.

I mention the name of this man, and also of the persons who perpetrated the deeds which I am about to relate, running the risk of being hurled back into interminable bondage—for I am yet a slave;—yet for the sake of the cause—for the sake of humanity, I will mention the names, and glory in running the risk. I have the gratification to know that if I fall by the utterance of truth in this matter, that if I shall be hurled back into bondage to gratify the slaveholder—to be killed by inches—that every drop of blood which I shall shed, every groan which I shall utter, every pain which shall rack my frame, every sob in which I shall indulge, shall be the instrument, under God, of tearing down the bloody pillar of Slavery, and of hastening the day of deliverance for three millions of my brethren in bondage.

I therefore tell the names of these bloody men, not because they are worse than other men would have been in their circumstances. No, they are bloody from necessity. Slavery makes it necessary for the slaveholder to commit all conceivable outrages upon the miserable slave. It is impossible to hold the slaves in bondage without this.

We had on the plantation an overseer, by the name of Austin Gore, a man who was highly respected as an overseer—proud, ambitious, cruel, artful, obdurate. Nearly every slave stood in the utmost dread and horror of that man. His eye flashed confusion amongst them. He never spoke but to command, nor commanded but to be obeyed. He was lavish with the whip, sparing with his word. I have seen that man tie up men by the two hands, and for two hours, at intervals, ply the lash. I have seen women stretched up on the limbs of trees, and their bare backs made bloody with the lash. One slave refused to be whipped by him—I need not tell you that he was a man, though black his features, degraded his condition. He had committed some trifling offence—for they whip for trifling offences—the slave refused to be whipped, and ran—he did not stand to and fight his master as I did once, and might do again—though I hope I shall not have occasion to do so—he ran and stood in a creek, and refused to come out. At length his master told him he would shoot him if he did not come out. Three calls were to be given him. The first, second, and third, were given, at each of which the slave stood his ground. Gore, equally determined and firm, raised his musket, and in an instant poor Derby was no more. He sank beneath the waves, and naught but the crimsoned waters marked the spot. Then a general outcry might be heard amongst us. Mr. Lloyd asked Gore why he had resorted to such a cruel measure. He replied, coolly, that he had done it from necessity; that the slave was setting a dangerous example, and that if he was permitted to be corrected and yet save his life, that the slaves would effectually rise and be freemen, and their masters be slaves. His defence was satisfactory. He remained on the plantation, and his fame went abroad. He still lives in St. Michaels, Talbot county, Maryland, and is now, I presume, as much respected, as though his guilty soul had never been stained with his brother's blood.

I might go on and mention other facts if time would permit. My own wife had a dear cousin who was terribly mangled in her sleep, while nursing the child of a Mrs. Hicks. Finding the girl asleep, Mrs. Hicks beat her to death with a billet of wood, and the woman has never been brought to justice. It is not a crime to kill a negro in Talbot county, Maryland, farther than it is a deprivation of a man's property. I used to know of one who boasted that he had killed two slaves, and with an oath would say, "I'm the only benefactor in the country."

Now, my friends, pardon me for having detained you so long; but let me tell you with regard to the feelings of the slave. The people at the North say—"Why don't you rise? If we were thus treated we would rise and throw off the yoke. We would wade knee deep in blood before we would endure the bondage." You'd rise up! Who are these that are asking for manhood in the slave, and who say that he has it not, because he does not rise? The very men who are ready by the Constitution to bring the strength of the nation to put us down! You, the people of New-York, the people of Massachusetts, of New England, of the whole Northern States, have sworn under God that we shall be slaves or die! And shall we three millions be taunted with a want of the love of freedom, by the very men who stand upon us and say, submit, or be crushed?

We don't ask you to engage in any physical warfare against the slaveholder. We only ask that in Massachusetts, and the several non-slaveholding States which maintain a union with the slaveholder—who stand with your heavy heels on the quivering heart-strings of the slave, that you will stand off. Leave us to take care of our masters. But here you come up to our masters and tell them that they ought to shoot us—to take away our wives and little ones—to sell our mothers into interminable bondage, and sever the tenderest ties. You say to us, if you dare to carry out the principles of our fathers, we'll shoot you down. Others may tamely submit; not I. You may put the chains upon me and fetter me, but I am not a slave, for my master who puts the chains upon me, shall stand in as much dread of me as I do of him. I ask you in the name of my three millions of brethren at the South. We know that we are unable to cope with you in numbers; you are numerically stronger, politically stronger, than we are—but we ask you if you will rend asunder the heart and [crush] the body of the slave? If so, you must do it at your own expense.

While you continue in the Union, you are as bad as the slaveholder. If you have thus wronged the poor black man, by stripping him of his freedom, how are you going to give evidence of your repentance? Undo what you have done. Do you say that the slave ought not to be free? These hands—are they not mine? This body—is it not mine? Again, I am your brother, white as you are. I'm your blood-kin. You don't get rid of me so easily. I mean to hold on to you. And in this land of liberty, I'm a slave. The twenty-six States that blaze forth on your flag, proclaim a compact to return me to bondage if I run away, and keep me in bondage if I submit. Wherever I go, under the aegis of your liberty, there I'm a slave. If I go to Lexington or Bunker Hill, there I'm a slave, chained in perpetual servitude. I may go to your deepest valley, to your highest mountain, I'm still a slave, and the bloodhound may chase me down.

Now I ask you if you are willing to have your country the hunting-ground of the slave. God says thou shalt not oppress: the Constitution says oppress: which will you serve, God or man? The American Anti-Slavery Society says God, and I am thankful for it. In the name of my brethren, to you, Mr. President, and the noble band who cluster around you, to you, who are scouted on every hand by priest, people, politician, Church, and State, to you I bring a thankful heart, and in the name of three millions of slaves, I offer you their gratitude for your faithful advocacy in behalf of the slave.

FREDERICK DOUGLASS

Letter to Thomas Auld

Letter, Frederick Douglass to Thomas Auld, September 3, 1848, published in The North Star, *September 8, 1848, and* The Liberator, *September 22, 1848. This version is reprinted from Philip S. Foner, ed.,* The Life and Writings of Frederick Douglass, *vol. 1 (New York: International Publishers, 1950), 336–43. This extraordinary letter by a former slave to his former master caused considerable controversy. Douglass later apologized (in 1849 and 1877) to Auld for some of the inaccuracies and bitterness in this letter, as well as in his autobiographies, especially regarding the claims against Auld's treatment of Betsey Bailey, Douglass's grandmother. The letter stands, though, as a prime example of confrontational antislavery propaganda.*

September 3d, 1848

Sir:

The long and intimate, though by no means friendly relation which unhappily subsisted between you and myself, leads me to hope that you will easily account for the great liberty which I now take in addressing you in this open and public manner. The same fact may possibly remove any disagreeable surprise which you may experience on again finding your name coupled with mine, in any other way than in an advertisement, accurately describing my person, and offering a large sum for my arrest. In thus dragging you again before the public, I am aware that I shall subject myself to no inconsiderable amount of censure. I shall probably be charged with an unwarrantable, if not a wanton and reckless disregard of the rights and proprieties of private life. There are those North as well as South who entertain a much higher respect for rights which are merely conventional, than they do for rights which are personal and essential. Not a few there are in our country, who, while they have no scruples against robbing the laborer of the hard earned results of his *patient industry,* will be shocked by the extremely indelicate manner of bringing your name before the public. Believing this to be the case, and wishing to meet every reasonable or plausible objection to my conduct, I will frankly state the ground upon which I justify myself in this instance, as well as on former occasions when I have thought proper to mention your name in public. All will agree that a man guilty of theft, robbery, or murder, has forfeited the right to concealment and private life; that the community have a right to subject such persons to the most complete exposure. However much they may desire retirement, and aim to conceal themselves and their movements from the popular gaze, the public have a right to ferret them out, and bring their conduct before the proper tribunals of the country for investigation. Sir, you will undoubtedly make the proper application of these generally admitted principles, and will easily see the light in which you are regarded by me. I will not therefore manifest ill temper, by calling you hard names. I know you to be a man of some intelligence, and can readily determine the precise estimate which I entertain of your character. I may therefore indulge in language which may seem to others indirect and ambiguous, and yet be quite well understood by yourself.

I have selected this day on which to address you, because it is the anniversary of my emancipation; and knowing of no better way, I am led to this as the best mode of celebrating that truly important event. Just ten years ago this beautiful September morning, yon bright sun beheld me a slave—a poor, degraded chattel—trembling at the sound of your voice, lamenting that I was a man, and wishing myself a brute. The hopes which I had treasured up for weeks of a safe and successful escape from your grasp, were powerfully confronted at this last hour by dark clouds of doubt and fear, making my person shake and my bosom to heave with the heavy contest between hope and fear. I have no words to describe to you the deep agony of soul which I experienced on that never to be forgotten morning—(for I left by daylight). I was making a leap in the dark. The probabilities, so far as I could by reason determine them, were stoutly against the undertaking. The preliminaries and precautions I had adopted previously, all worked badly. I was like one going to war without weapons—ten chances of defeat to one of victory. One in whom I had confided, and one who had promised me assistance, appalled by fear at the trial hour, deserted me, thus leaving the responsibility of success or failure solely with myself. You, sir, can never know my feelings. As I look back to them, I can scarcely realize that I have passed through a scene so trying. Trying however as they were, and gloomy as was the prospect, thanks be to the Most High, who is ever the God of the oppressed, at the moment which was to determine my whole earthly career. His grace was sufficient, my mind was made up. I embraced the golden opportunity, took the morning tide at the flood, and a free man, young, active and strong, is the result.

I have often thought I should like to explain to you the grounds upon which I have justified myself in running away from you. I am almost ashamed to do so now, for by this time you may have discovered them yourself. I will, however, glance at them. When yet but a child about six years old, I imbibed the determination to run away. The very first mental effort that I now remember on my part, was an attempt to solve the mystery, Why am I a slave? and with this question my youthful mind was troubled for many days, pressing upon me more heavily at times than others. When I saw the slave-driver whip a slave woman, cut the blood out of her neck, and heard her piteous cries, I went away into the corner of the fence, wept and pondered over the mystery. I had, through some medium, I know not what, got some idea of God, the Creator of all mankind, the black and the white, and that he had made the blacks to serve the whites as slaves. How he could do this and be *good,* I could not tell. I was not satisfied with this theory, which made God responsible for slavery, for it pained me greatly, and I have wept over it long and often. At one time, your first wife, Mrs. Lucretia, heard me singing and saw me shedding tears, and asked of me the matter, but I was afraid to tell her. I was puzzled with this question, till one night, while sitting in the kitchen, I heard some of the old slaves talking of their parents having been stolen from Africa by white men, and were sold here as slaves. The whole mystery was solved at once. Very soon after this my aunt Jinny and uncle Noah ran away, and the great noise made about it by your father-in-law, made me for the first time acquainted with the fact, that there were free States as well as slave States. From that time, I resolved

that I would some day run away. The morality of the act, I dispose as follows: I am myself; you are yourself; we are two distinct persons, equal persons. What you are, I am. You are a man, and so am I. God created both, and made us separate beings. I am not by nature bound to you, or you to me. Nature does not make your existence depend upon me, or mine to depend upon yours. I cannot walk upon your legs, or you upon mine. I cannot breathe for you, or you for me; I must breathe for myself, and you for yourself. We are distinct persons, and are each equally provided with faculties necessary to our individual existence. In leaving you, I took nothing but what belonged to me, and in no way lessened your means for obtaining an *honest* living. Your faculties remained yours, and mine became useful to their rightful owner. I therefore see no wrong in any part of the transaction. It is true, I went off secretly, but that was more your fault than mine. Had I let you into the secret, you would have defeated the enterprise entirely; but for this, I should have been really glad to have made you acquainted with my intentions to leave.

You may perhaps want to know how I like my present condition. I am free to say, I greatly prefer it to that which I occupied in Maryland. I am, however, by no means prejudiced against the State as such. Its geography, climate, fertility and products, are such as to make it a very desirable abode for any man; and but for the existence of slavery there, it is not impossible that I might again take up my abode in that State. It is not that I love Maryland less, but freedom more. You will be surprised to learn that people at the North labor under the strange delusion that if the slaves were emancipated at the South, they would flock to the North. So far from this being the case, in that event, you would see many old and familiar faces back again to the South. The fact is, there are few here who would not return to the South in the event of emancipation. We want to live in the land of our birth, and to lay our bones by the side of our fathers'; and nothing short of an intense love of personal freedom keeps us from the South. For the sake of this, most of us would live on a crust of bread and a cup of cold water.

Since I left you, I have had a rich experience. I have occupied stations which I never dreamed of when a slave. Three out of the ten years since I left you, I spent as a common laborer on the wharves of New Bedford, Massachusetts. It was there I earned my first free dollar. It was mine. I could spend it as I pleased. I could buy hams or herring with it, without asking any odds of any body. That was a precious dollar to me. You remember when I used to make seven or eight, or even nine dollars a week in Baltimore, you would take every cent of it from me every Saturday night, saying that I belonged to you, and my earnings also. I never liked this conduct on your part—to say the best, I thought it a little mean. I would not have served you so. But let that pass. I was a little awkward about counting money in New

England fashion when I first landed in New Bedford. I like to have betrayed myself several times. I caught myself saying phip, for fourpence; and at one time a man actually charged me with being a runaway, whereupon I was silly enough to become one by running away from him, for I was greatly afraid he might adopt measures to get me again into slavery, a condition I then dreaded more than death.

I soon, however, learned to count money, as well as to make it, and got on swimmingly. I married soon after leaving you: in fact, I was engaged to be married before I left you; and instead of finding my companion a burden, she was truly a helpmeet. She went to live at service, and I to work on the wharf, and though we toiled hard the first winter, we never lived more happily. After remaining in New Bedford for three years, I met with Wm. Lloyd Garrison, a person of whom you have *possibly* heard, as he is pretty generally known among slaveholders. He put it into my head that I might make myself serviceable to the cause of the slave by devoting a portion of my time to telling my own sorrows, and those of other slaves which had come under my observation. This was the commencement of a higher state of existence than any to which I had ever aspired. I was thrown into society the most pure, enlightened and benevolent that the country affords. Among these I have never forgotten you, but have invariably made you the topic of conversation—thus giving you all the notoriety I could do. I need not tell you that the opinion formed of you in these circles, is far from being favorable. They have little respect for your honesty, and less for your religion.

But I was going on to relate to you something of my interesting experience. I had not long enjoyed the excellent society to which I have referred, before the light of its excellence exerted a beneficial influence on my mind and heart. Much of my early dislike of white persons was removed, and their manners, habits and customs, so entirely unlike what I had been used to in the kitchen-quarters on the plantations of the South, fairly charmed me, and gave me a strong disrelish for the coarse and degrading customs of my former condition. I therefore made an effort so to improve my mind and deportment, as to be somewhat fitted to the station to which I seemed almost providentially called. The transition from degradation to respectability was indeed great, and to get from one to the other without carrying some marks of one's former condition, is truly a difficult matter. I would not have you think that I am now entirely clear of all plantation peculiarities, but my friends here, while they entertain the strongest dislike to them, regard me with that charity to which my past life somewhat entitles me, so that my condition in this respect is exceedingly pleasant. So far as my domestic affairs are concerned, I can boast of as comfortable a dwelling as your own. I have an industrious and neat companion, and four dear children—the oldest a girl of nine years, and three fine boys, the oldest eight, the next six, and the youngest four years old. The three oldest are now going regularly to school—two can read and write, and the other can spell with tolerable correctness words of two syllables: Dear fellows! they are all in comfortable beds, and are sound asleep, perfectly secure under my own roof. There are no slaveholders here to rend my heart by snatching them from my arms, or blast a mother's dearest hopes by tearing them from her bosom. These dear children are ours—not to work up into rice, sugar and tobacco, but to watch over, regard, and protect, and to rear them up in the nurture and admonition of the gospel—to train them up in the paths of wisdom and virtue, and, as far as we can to make them useful to the world and to themselves. Oh! sir, a slaveholder never appears to me so completely an agent of hell, as when I think of and look upon my dear children. It is then that my feelings rise above my control. I meant to have said more with respect to my own prosperity and happiness, but thoughts and feelings which this recital has quickened unfits me to proceed further in that direction. The grim horrors of slavery rise in all their ghastly terror before me, the wails of millions pierce my heart, and chill my blood. I remember the chain, the gag, the bloody whip, the death-like gloom overshadowing the broken spirit of the fettered bondman, the appalling liability of his being torn away from wife and children, and sold like a beast in the market. Say not that this is a picture of fancy. You well know that I wear stripes on my back inflicted by your direction; and that you, while we were brothers in the same church, caused this right hand, with which I am now penning this letter, to be closely tied to my left, and my person dragged at the pistol's mouth, fifteen miles, from the Bay side to Easton to be sold like a beast in the market, for the alleged crime of intending to escape from your possession. All this and more you remember, and know to be perfectly true, not only of yourself, but of nearly all of the slaveholders around you.

At this moment, you are probably the guilty holder of at least three of my own dear sisters, and my only brother in bondage. These you regard as your property. They are recorded on your ledger, or perhaps have been sold to human flesh mongers, with a view to filling your own ever-hungry purse. Sir, I desire to know how and where these dear sisters are. Have you sold them? or are they still in your possession? What has become of them? are they living or dead? And my dear old grand-mother, whom you turned out like an old horse, to die in the woods—is she still alive? Write and let me know all about them. If my grandmother be still alive, she is of no service to you, for by this time she must be nearly eighty years old—too old to be cared for by one to whom she has ceased to be of service, send her to me at Rochester, or bring her to Philadelphia, and it shall be the crowning happiness of my life to take care of her in her old age. Oh! she was to me a mother, and a father, so far as hard toil for my comfort could make her such. Send me my grandmother! that I may watch over and take care of her in her old age. And my sisters, let me know all about them. I would write to them, and learn all I want to know of them, without disturbing you in any way, but that, through your unrighteous conduct, they have been entirely deprived of the power to read and write. You have kept them in utter ignorance, and have therefore robbed them of the sweet enjoyments of writing or receiving letters from absent friends and relatives. Your wickedness and cruelty committed in this respect on your fellow-creatures, are greater than all the stripes you have laid upon my back, or theirs. It is an outrage upon the soul—a war upon the immortal spirit, and one for which you must give account at the bar of our common Father and Creator.

The responsibility which you have assumed in this regard is truly awful—and how you could stagger under it these many years is marvellous. Your mind must have become darkened, your heart hardened, your conscience seared and petrified, or you would have long since thrown off the accursed load and sought relief at the hands of a sin-forgiving God. How, let me ask, would you look upon me, were I some dark night in company with a band of hardened villains, to enter the precincts of your elegant dwelling and seize the person of your own lovely daughter Amanda, and carry her off from your family, friends and all the loved ones of her youth—make her my slave—compel her to work, and I take her wages—place her name on my ledger as property—disregard her personal rights—fetter the powers of her immortal soul by denying her the right and privilege of learning to read and write—feed her coarsely—clothe her scantily, and whip her on the naked back occasionally; more and still more horrible, leave her unprotected—a degraded victim to the brutal lust of fiendish overseers, who would pollute, blight, and blast her fair soul—rob her of all dignity—destroy her virtue, and annihilate all in her person the graces that adorn the character of virtuous womanhood? I ask how would you regard me, if such were my conduct? Oh! the vocabulary of the damned would not afford a word sufficiently infernal, to express your idea of my God-provoking wickedness. Yet sir, your treatment of my beloved sisters is in all essential points, precisely like the case I have now supposed. Damning as would be such a deed on my part, it would be no more so than that which you have committed against me and my sisters.

I will now bring this letter to a close, you shall hear from me again unless you let me hear from you. I intend to make use of you as a weapon with which to assail the system of slavery—as a means of concentrating public attention on the system, and deepening their horror of trafficking in the souls and bodies of men. I shall make use of you as a means of exposing the character of the American church and clergy—and as a means of bringing this guilty nation with yourself to repentance. In doing this I entertain no malice towards you personally. There is no roof under which you would be more safe than mine, and there is nothing in my house which you might need for your comfort, which I would not readily grant. Indeed, I should esteem it a privilege, to set you an example as to how mankind ought to treat each other.

I am your fellow man, but not your slave,

Frederick Douglass

FREDERICK DOUGLASS

What to the Slave Is the Fourth of July?

"What to the Slave Is the Fourth of July?" speech by Frederick Douglass, delivered in Corinthian Hall, Rochester, New York, to an audience of nearly 600 people, July 5, 1852. This excerpted version is the one Douglass reprinted as an appendix in his 1855 autobiography, My Bondage and My Freedom. *The complete text can be found in John W. Blassingame, ed.,* The Frederick Douglass Papers, *series 1, vol. 2 (New Haven: Yale University Press, 1982), 359–88.*

EXTRACT FROM AN ORATION AT ROCHESTER, JULY 5, 1852

Fellow-Citizens—pardon me, and allow me to ask, why am I called upon to speak here to-day? What have I, or those I represent, to do with your national independence? Are the great principles of political freedom and of natural justice, embodied in that Declaration of Independence, extended to us? and am I, therefore, called upon to bring our humble offering to the national altar, and to confess the benefits, and express devout gratitude for the blessings, resulting from your independence to us?

Would to God, both for your sakes and ours, that an affirmative answer could be truthfully returned to these questions! Then would my task be light, and my burden easy and ˌdelightful. For who is there so cold that a nation's sympathy could not warm him? Who so obdurate and dead to the claims of gratitude, that would not thankfully acknowledge such priceless benefits? Who so stolid and selfish, that would not give his voice to swell the hallelujah of a nation's jubilee, when the chains of servitude had been torn from his limbs? I am not that man. In a case like that, the dumb might eloquently speak, and the "lame man leap as an hart."[1]

But, such is not the state of the case. I say it with a sad sense of the disparity between us. I am not included within the pale of this glorious anniversary! Your high independence only reveals the immeasurable distance between us. The blessings in which you this day rejoice, are not enjoyed in common. The rich inheritance of justice, liberty, prosperity, and independence, bequeathed by your fathers, is shared by you, not by me. The sunlight that brought life and healing to you, has brought stripes and death to me. This Fourth of July is *yours,* not *mine. You* may rejoice, *I* must mourn. To drag a man in fetters into the grand illuminated temple of liberty, and call upon him to join you in joyous anthems, were inhuman mockery and sacrilegious irony. Do you mean, citizens, to mock me, by asking me to speak to-day? If so, there is a parallel to your conduct. And let me warn you that it is dangerous to copy the example of a nation whose crimes, towering up to heaven, were thrown down by the breath of the Almighty, burying that nation in irrecoverable ruin! I can to-day take up the plaintive lament of a peeled and woe-smitten people.

"By the rivers of Babylon, there we sat down. Yea! we wept when we remembered Zion. We hanged our harps upon the willows in the midst thereof. For there, they that carried us away captive, required of us a song; and they who wasted us required of us mirth, saying, Sing us one of the songs of Zion. How can we sing the Lord's song in a strange land? If I forget thee, O Jerusalem, let my right hand forget her cunning. If I do not remember thee, let my tongue cleave to the roof of my mouth."[2]

Fellow-citizens, above your national, tumultuous joy, I hear the mournful wail of millions, whose chains, heavy and grievous yesterday, are to-day rendered more intolerable by the jubilant shouts that reach them. If I do forget, if I do not faithfully remember those bleeding children of sorrow this day, "may my right hand forget her cunning, and may my tongue cleave to the roof of my mouth!" To forget them, to pass lightly over their wrongs, and to chime in with the popular theme, would be treason most scandalous and shocking, and would make me a reproach before God and the world. My subject then, fellow-citizens, is AMERICAN SLAVERY. I shall see this day and its popular characteristics from the slave's point of view. Standing there, identified with the American bondman, making his wrongs mine, I do not hesitate to declare, with all my soul, that the character and conduct of this nation never looked blacker to me than on this Fourth of July. Whether we turn to the declarations of the past, or to the professions of the present, the conduct of the nation seems equally hideous and revolting. America is false to the past, false to the present, and solemnly binds herself to be false to the future. Standing with God and the crushed and bleeding slave on this occasion, I will, in the name of humanity which is outraged, in the name of liberty which is fettered, in the name of the constitution and the bible, which are disregarded and trampled upon, dare to call in question and to denounce, with all the emphasis I can command, everything that serves to perpetuate slavery—the great sin and shame of America! "I will not equivocate; I will not excuse;"[3] I will use the severest language I can command; and yet not one word shall escape me that any man, whose judgment is not blinded by prejudice, or who is not at heart a slaveholder, shall not confess to be right and just.

But I fancy I hear some one of my audience say, it is just in this circumstance that you and your brother abolitionists fail to make a favorable impression on the public mind. Would you argue more, and denounce less, would you persuade more and rebuke less, your cause would be much more likely to succeed. But, I submit, where all is plain there is nothing to be argued. What point in the anti-slavery creed would you have me argue? On what branch of the subject do the people of this country need light? Must I undertake to prove that the slave is a man? That point is conceded already. Nobody doubts it. The slaveholders themselves acknowledge it in the enactment of laws for their government. They acknowledge it when they punish disobedience on the part of the slave. There are seventy-two crimes in the state of Virginia, which, if committed by a black man, (no matter how ignorant he be,) subject him to the punishment of death; while only two of these same crimes will subject a white man to the like punishment. What is this but the acknowledgment that the slave is a moral, intellectual, and responsible being. The manhood of the slave is conceded. It is admitted in the fact that southern statute books are covered with enactments forbidding, under severe fines and penalties, the teaching of the slave to read or write. When you can point to any such laws, in reference to the beasts of the field, then I may consent to argue the manhood of the slave. When the dogs in your streets, when the fowls of the air, when the cattle on your hills, when the fish of the sea, and the reptiles that crawl, shall be unable to distinguish the slave from a brute, then will I argue with you that the slave is a man!

For the present, it is enough to affirm the equal manhood of the negro race. Is it not astonishing that, while we are plowing, planting, and reaping, using all kinds of mechanical tools, erecting houses, constructing bridges, building ships, working in metals of brass, iron, copper, silver, and gold; that, while we are reading, writing, and cyphering, acting as clerks, merchants, and secretaries, having among us lawyers, doctors, ministers, poets, authors, editors, orators, and teachers; that, while we are engaged in all manner of enterprises common to other men—digging gold in California, capturing the whale in the Pacific, feeding sheep and cattle on the hillside, living, moving, acting, thinking, planning, living in families as husbands, wives, and children, and, above all, confessing and worshiping the christian's God, and looking hopefully for life and immortality beyond the grave,—we are called upon to prove that we are men!

Would you have me argue that man is entitled to liberty? that he is the rightful owner of his own body? You have already declared it. Must I argue the wrongfulness of slavery? Is that a question for republicans? Is it to be settled by the rules of logic and argumentation, as a matter beset with great difficulty, involving a doubtful application of the principle of justice, hard to be understood? How should I look to-day in the presence of Americans, dividing and subdividing a discourse, to show that men have a natural right to freedom, speaking of it relatively and positively, negatively and affirmatively? To do so, would be to make myself ridiculous, and to offer an insult to your understanding. There is not a man beneath the canopy of heaven that does not know that slavery is wrong *for him*.

What! am I to argue that it is wrong to make men brutes, to rob them of their liberty, to work them without wages, to keep them ignorant of their relations to their fellow-men, to beat them with sticks, to flay their flesh with the lash, to load their limbs with irons, to hunt them with dogs, to sell them at auction, to sunder their families, to knock out their teeth, to burn their flesh, to starve them into obedience and submission to their masters? Must I argue that a system, thus marked with blood and stained with pollution, is wrong? No; I will not. I have better employment for my time and strength than such arguments would imply.

What, then, remains to be argued? Is it that slavery is not divine; that God did not establish it; that our doctors of divinity are mistaken? There is blasphemy in the thought. That which is inhuman cannot be divine. Who can reason on such a proposition! They that can, may; I cannot. The time for such argument is past.

At a time like this, scorching irony, not convincing argument, is needed. Oh! had I the ability, and could I reach the nation's ear, I would to-day pour out a fiery stream of biting ridicule, blasting reproach, withering sarcasm, and stern rebuke. For it is not light that is needed, but fire; it is not the gentle shower, but thunder. We need the storm, the whirlwind and the earthquake.

The feeling of the nation must be quickened; the conscience of the nation must be roused; the propriety of the nation must be startled; the hypocrisy of the nation must be exposed; and its crimes against God and man must be proclaimed and denounced.

What to the American slave is your Fourth of July? I answer, a day that reveals to him, more than all other days in the year, the gross injustice and cruelty to which he is the constant victim. To him, your celebration is a sham; your boasted liberty, an unholy license; your national greatness, swelling vanity; your sounds of rejoicing are empty and heartless; your denunciations of tyrants, brass-fronted impudence; your shouts of liberty and equality, hollow mockery; your prayers and hymns, your sermons and thanksgivings, with all your religious parade and solemnity, are to him mere bombast, fraud, deception, impiety, and hypocrisy—a thin veil to cover up crimes which would disgrace a nation of savages. There is not a nation on the earth guilty of practices more shocking and bloody, than are the people of these United States, at this very hour.

Go where you may, search where you will, roam through all the monarchies and despotisms of the old world, travel through South America, search out every abuse, and when you have found the last, lay your facts by the side of the every-day practices of this nation, and you will say with me, that, for revolting barbarity and shameless hypocrisy, America reigns without a rival.

NOTES

[1] The biblical reference is Isaiah 35:6.

[2] Douglass draws directly from Psalms 137:1–6.

[3] Douglass quotes from William Lloyd Garrison's opening editorial in the first issue of *The Liberator,* 1 Jan. 1831: "I am in earnest—I will not equivocate—I will not excuse—I will not retreat a single inch—and *I will be heard.*"

Frederick Douglass, photographed shortly after the Civil War

A Douglass Chronology
(1818–1895)

At the end of Frederick Douglass's third autobiography, *The Life and Times of Frederick Douglass* (1881, rev. 1892), he declares that he had "lived several lives in one: first, the life of slavery; secondly, the life of a fugitive from slavery; thirdly, the life of comparative freedom; fourthly, the life of conflict and battle; and fifthly, the life of victory, if not complete, at least assured."[1] With an autobiographer's concentration on the self, Douglass wanted to demonstrate the struggle and achievement in his life. He had suffered and overcome, we are told. He had persevered through hopelessness, led his people through a trial, and in the end reached at least a personal triumph. These are the images of an aging man summing up his life and attempting to control his historical reputation. In Douglass's categories we see his self-image as the fugitive slave risen to racial and national leader, the person and the nation regenerated. Like all great autobiographers, Douglass was trying to order, even control, the passage of time, and thereby make sense of his own history. As he imagined his chronology, he discovered, as did the later classic autobiographer Vladimir Nabokov, that "the prison of time is spherical and without exits."[2]

As a source of historical truth, autobiography must be interpreted with caution, but the stages Douglass gave his life are instructive. They represent many of the turning points that define his illustrious career. No simple chronology can convey the deeper meanings in such an eventful life. Douglass may have said this best himself in a speech entitled "Life Pictures," first delivered in 1861. The final lines of that speech represent perhaps his most humanistic, if indirect, autobiographical statement: "We live in deeds, not years, in thoughts not breaths, in feeling, not fingers on a dial. We should count time by heartthrobs; he most lives who thinks the most, feels the noblest, acts the best."[3]

"THE LIFE OF SLAVERY" (1818–1838)

1818, February: Frederick Augustus Washington Bailey born on the Holme Hill farm on Tuckahoe Creek, Talbot County, Maryland.

1824: Sent to live on Lloyd plantation, Wye River, in house of his master, Aaron Anthony.

1825: Sees his mother, Harriet Bailey, for the last time; she dies in early 1826.

1826: Sent to live in Baltimore with Hugh and Sophia Auld.

1826–27: Aaron Anthony dies; Frederick sent back to Eastern Shore to be divided as the property of Anthony's heirs; awarded to Thomas Auld and sent back to Baltimore after one month.

1827: Sophia Auld helps Frederick learn to read.

1831: Undergoes religious conversion and discovers the book *The Columbian Orator.*

1832: Sister Sarah is sold away to Mississippi, one of fifteen close relatives "sold South" during Frederick's childhood.

1833: Sent back to St. Michaels, Eastern Shore, to live with his owner, Thomas Auld.

1834, January: Hired out to Edward Covey, suffers many beatings. The famous fight with Covey occurs in August.

1835, January: Hired out to William Freeland as a field hand; conducts a Sabbath school among fellow slaves.

1836, April: Escape plot fails, jailed in Easton, Maryland; sent back to Baltimore by Thomas Auld.

1836–38: Works as caulker in Baltimore shipyards; beaten by white apprentices; meets Anna Murray.

1838, September 3: Escapes from slavery by train and boat; marries Anna in New York City on September 15; they settle in New Bedford, Massachusetts; chooses new name, Douglass.

"THE LIFE OF A FUGITIVE FROM SLAVERY" (1838–1846)

1838–39: Works as day laborer and caulker in New Bedford.

1839: Speaks at meeting of New Bedford blacks against African colonization; becomes licensed preacher in African Methodist Episcopal Zion church; daughter Rosetta born June 24.

1840–41: Son Lewis born October 9; William Lloyd Garrison discovers Douglass as a speaker at an antislavery meeting, invites him to convention.

1841, August: Delivers three speeches at Massachusetts antislavery convention on Nantucket Island; hired as a lecturer by Garrison's organization.

1841–43: Travels extensively in New England, New York, and across the North as an abolitionist speaker, "telling his story" as a slave and attacking religious hypocrisy as well as northern racism; draws huge crowds to his orations; beaten badly in Pendleton, Indiana, in September 1843, suffers broken hand; son Frederick born March 3, 1842.

1844–45: Writes the *Narrative* at home in Lynn, Massachusetts; son Charles born October 21, 1844.

1845, May 28: *Narrative* is published in Boston, revealing his full identity.

1845, August–December: Sails for the British Isles aboard the *Cambria,* where passengers threaten to throw him overboard if he delivers an abolitionist speech; tours Ireland for three months speaking to large audiences and selling a newly published Dublin edition of the *Narrative.*

1846: Tours Scotland and England in a much celebrated lecturing campaign; his freedom purchased for 150 pounds ($711) by British antislavery friends; his manumission papers are filed in Baltimore.

"THE LIFE OF COMPARATIVE FREEDOM" (1847–1855)

1847: Returns to the United States; moves to Rochester, New York, and founds his own newspaper, the *North Star,* against the opposition of Garrison and Wendell Phillips; first issue of *North Star* published December 3.

1848, February: First meets John Brown in Springfield, Massachusetts.

1848, July: Attends and speaks at first Women's Rights Convention, Seneca Falls, New York; begins long association with women's rights movement.

1848–50: Julia Griffiths, an Englishwoman Douglass met in 1845, moves to America, lives in the Douglass home in Rochester, serves as editorial assistant, fund-raiser, and valued friend; Douglass becomes object of resentment and rumormongering by Garrisonians.

1849: Daughter Annie born March 22.

1850–51: Breaks with Garrisonians over issues of political action, the antislavery interpretation of the Constitution, and his own professional independence; begins close association with upstate New York abolitionist Gerrit Smith.

1851: Changes name of newspaper to *Frederick Douglass' Paper;* aids three Maryland fugitive slaves escaping to Canada who had violently resisted recapture by their former master by killing him in Christiana, Pennsylvania.

1851–55: Becomes increasingly involved in antislavery politics through the Liberty and Free-Soil parties; continues abolitionist lecturing across the North.

1852, July: Delivers famous Fourth of July speech in Rochester, New York, one of the greatest American literary works about the meaning of slavery and freedom in a republic.

1855: Publishes *My Bondage and My Freedom,* his second and more thorough autobiography.

"THE LIFE OF CONFLICT AND BATTLE" (1855–1865)

1854–56: Increasingly supports the right of slaves and their defenders to violent resistance against slaveholders and slave catchers.

1856: Supports the Republican candidate, John C. Frémont, for president, beginning an ambivalent but increasingly positive association with the new antislavery party.

1857: Condemns and calls for political resistance to the Dred Scott decision.

1858, February: John Brown stays for a month in Douglass's home in Rochester while making plans for his raid into Virginia and incitement of slave revolt; Douglass supports Brown's vague plans.

1859: Meets with Brown near Chambersburg, Pennsylvania, in August; refuses to join the ill-fated raid; flees the country in the wake of Brown's raid in October as he is sought by U.S. marshals as an accomplice; sails to England via Canada, staying six months.

1860, May: Returns to America after the death of his eleven-year-old daughter, Annie.

1860: Supports and works for Abraham Lincoln's election to the presidency; disappointed that a property requirement for black voters in New York State is upheld by the voters; attacked by a prosouthern mob at a meeting to commemorate John Brown in Boston in December.

1861: Welcomes secession, sees the hope of emancipation in the crisis of disunion and the outbreak of the Civil War, and demands enlistment of black troops in Union armies.

1861–62: In editorials and speeches such as "The Slaveholder's Rebellion," becomes an aggressive war propagandist for the Union cause.

1862, December 31: Speaks and leads singing at celebration in Boston's Tremont Temple as the Emancipation Proclamation becomes law.

1863, February–July: Travels across the North recruiting more than one hundred members of the black regiment, the Fifty-fourth Massachusetts; sons Lewis and Charles are first recruits.

1863, July–August: Ceases recruiting in protest of discrimination against black soldiers in pay, rank, and other treatment. Meets in Washington with President Lincoln and Secretary of War Edwin Stanton. Ends sixteen years of publication of newspaper, now called *Douglass Monthly;* expects an army commission that never comes.

1863–64: Travels across the North, speaks to thousands with new speech, "The Mission of the War," arguing that the conflict must become a "national regeneration," a second American Revolution, a new founding rooted in freedom and dedicated to racial equality.

1864: Nearly opposes Lincoln's reelection but reverses himself; called to White House in August to advise the president on election and securing emancipation; works for Republican victory and prosecution of the war.

1865: Attends Lincoln's second inauguration in March; speaks at many "Jubilee meetings" in black communities across the North, and at large public gathering in Rochester in April, in wake of Lincoln's assassination; calls his fellow citizens "countrymen" and "kin."

"THE LIFE OF VICTORY, IF NOT COMPLETE, AT LEAST ASSURED" (1865–1895)

1865–66: Supports radical Republican Reconstruction plans; part of black delegation that meets with President Andrew Johnson to criticize his policies; strongly advocates black suffrage.

1867: Reunion, after forty years, with brother Perry, who had been "sold South" from Maryland. Builds Perry's family a house in Rochester.

1868, August–October: Campaigns for Ulysses S. Grant for president.

1868–69: Despite its limitations, rejoices in the passage of the Fifteenth Amendment; breaks with women's rights movement over their opposition to the amendment's silence on women's suffrage.

1870: Purchases and becomes editor of newspaper *New National Era* in Washington, D.C.

1871: Appointed by Grant as assistant secretary of commission to Santo Domingo; supports Grant's plans to annex the Caribbean island.

1872: Rochester home destroyed by fire, arson suspected, many important papers lost; family moves to Washington, D.C.

1870s: Struggles unsuccessfully to combine advocacy of economic uplift for the freedpeople with demands for political rights.

1874: Named president of ill-fated Freedmen's Bank, which closes under his leadership; ceases publication of *New National Era.*

1876–77: Becomes stalwart Republican party functionary; appointed U.S. marshal for the District of Columbia by President Rutherford Hayes.

1877: Returns to St. Michaels, Maryland, after forty-one years; meets with former owner Thomas Auld on Auld's deathbed.

1878: Purchases Cedar Hill, a fifteen-acre estate in Anacostia, D.C.

1881: Appointed recorder of deeds for District of Columbia by President James Garfield; third autobiography, *The Life and Times of Frederick Douglass,* published.

1870s–'80s: Travels widely from New England to the Great Plains with most popular lecture, "Self-made Men"; speaks at numerous emancipation anniversaries, G.A.R. post meetings, black churches, and civic and national events about the meaning and memory of the Civil War from a black abolitionist perspective.

1882, August: Anna, wife of forty-four years, dies after long illness.

1884, January: Marries Helen Pitts, his white former secretary and Mt. Holyoke College graduate; marriage causes considerable controversy in family and black community.

1885–87:   Tours England, France, Italy, Egypt, and Greece with Helen.

1889:   Appointed minister and consul general to Haiti by President Benjamin Harrison; remains in post until July 1891; resigns in protest of U.S. maneuvering to seize Môle Saint Nicolas.

1892:   Publishes updated version of third autobiography, *The Life and Times of Frederick Douglass;* the book does not sell well.

1892–93:   Serves as commissioner for the Republic of Haiti pavilion at the World's Columbian Exposition in Chicago; collaborates with antilynching activist and journalist Ida B. Wells to issue *The Reason Why the Colored American is Not in the World's Columbian Exposition.*

1894, January: Delivers last major speech, "The Lessons of the Hour," a bitter analysis and denunciation of lynching in America, at the Metropolitan African Methodist Episcopal Church, in Washington, D.C.

1895, February 20:   Dies of heart attack at Cedar Hill; funeral services at Metropolitan A.M.E. Church on February 25; burial in Mt. Hope Cemetery, Rochester, February 26.

NOTES

[1] *The Life and Times of Frederick Douglass* (1882; rpt. New York: Collier Books, 1962), 479.
[2] Vladimir Nabokov, *Speak, Memory: An Autobiography Revisited* (1947; rev. ed. New York: Random House, 1966), 20.
[3] Frederick Douglass, lecture, "Life Pictures," at the Parker Fraternity Course, Boston, winter 1861, in Frederick Douglass Papers (Library of Congress), reel 14, 28.

Questions for Consideration

1. In both specific and general terms, what is the argument of William Lloyd Garrison's preface to Douglass's *Narrative?*

2. As a historical source, what does Douglass's *Narrative* reveal about the lives, culture, and psychological struggles of American slaves?

3. In what ways is Douglass's *Narrative* a work of abolitionist propaganda? In what ways is it a historical source on the nature and arguments of the abolition movement in antebellum America?

4. How is Douglass's *Narrative* an example of the will to be known (or the will to power) as the will to write? In other words, why were literacy and reading so important to Douglass?

5. In what ways might this book be compared with the Book of Psalms in the Bible? What are some other biblical images and influences evident in the text?

6. Critically discuss the following themes in Douglass's *Narrative:* home, power, violence, friendship, mind, manhood.

7. Critically discuss how Douglass's *Narrative* might be read as a meditation on the multiple meanings of *freedom.*

8. Is an autobiography like Douglass's *Narrative* to be trusted as a source of historical truth and understanding? Why or why not?

9. How does Douglass portray slaveholders? What strategy do these portrayals have in his story?

10. What is the argument of Douglass's appendix?

11. What is the meaning of the full title of the *Narrative?*

12. What does Douglass have to say about the consequences of slavery for Americans, black and white, North and South?

13. In what sense can it be said that Douglass had already lived at least

"two lives" by the time he wrote the *Narrative*? Can you find places in the text where he seems to move between two spheres of time: the past described and the present in which he was writing? How is this a dilemma in the uses of memory by any autobiographer? by any of us as we seek to know, reconstruct, and learn from the past?

14. Is Douglass's book more a work of imaginative literature than of history, or the other way around?

15. How effectively does Douglass use *irony* in telling his story, and in creating the self he constructs in the *Narrative*?

Selected Bibliography

AUTOBIOGRAPHIES

Narrative of the Life of Frederick Douglass, An American Slave, Written by Himself (1845).
My Bondage and My Freedom (1855).
The Life and Times of Frederick Douglass (1881, rev. 1892).

COLLECTIONS OF DOUGLASS'S WRITINGS, EDITORIALS, AND SPEECHES

Blassingame, John W., ed. *The Frederick Douglass Papers,* 4 vols. New Haven: Yale University Press, 1979–.
Foner, Philip S., ed. *The Life and Writings of Frederick Douglass,* 5 vols., New York: International Publishers, 1950.
Meyer, Michael. *Frederick Douglass: The Narrative and Selected Writings.* New York: Modern Library, 1984.
Foner, Philip S., ed. *Frederick Douglass on Women's Rights.* Westport, Conn.: Greenwood Press, 1976.

COLLECTIONS OF ESSAYS ABOUT DOUGLASS

Andrews, William L., ed. *Critical Essays on Frederick Douglass.* Boston: G. K. Hall, 1991.
Sundquist, Eric J., ed. *Frederick Douglass: New Literary and Historical Essays.* Cambridge: Cambridge University Press, 1990.

BIOGRAPHIES

McFeely, William S. *Frederick Douglass.* New York: W.W. Norton, 1991.
Blight, David W. *Frederick Douglass' Civil War: Keeping Faith in Jubilee.* Baton Rouge: Louisiana State University Press, 1989.
Martin, Waldo E. *The Mind of Frederick Douglass.* Chapel Hill: University of North Carolina Press, 1984.

Preston, Dickson J. *Young Frederick Douglass: The Maryland Years.* Baltimore: Johns Hopkins University Press, 1980.

Huggins, Nathan Irvin. *Slave and Citizen: The Life of Frederick Douglass.* Boston: Little, Brown, 1980.

Walker, Peter F. *Moral Choices: Memory, Desire, and Imagination in Nineteenth Century American Abolition.* Baton Rouge: Louisiana State University Press, 1978.

Bontemps, Arna. *Free at Last: The Life of Frederick Douglass.* New York: Dodd, Mead, 1971.

Foner, Philip S. *Frederick Douglass.* Citadel, 1964.

Quarles, Benjamin. *Frederick Douglass.* 1948; rpt. New York: Atheneum, 1968.

Index

fate of, 113n. 46
fears loss of reputation, 79–80
habit of surprising slaves, 72–73
loses fight with Douglass, 78, 79
rents Douglass from owner, 70–71
Crimes
 against slaves, 51–53
 death penalty for slaves, 143
Cruelty
 incidents noted by Garrison, 34
 of Austin Gore, 51–53
 of Mrs. Hamilton toward slaves, 58–59
 of Thomas Auld, 67, 68, 70

Denby, Bill, 52, 111n. 18
Douglass, Anna (Murray), 99–100, 115n. 63
Douglass, Frederick
 ancestry of, 2–3
 arrives in Baltimore, 56
 as rhetorical man, 4
 as traveling lecturer, 5
 birthplace of, 39
 brief life history of, 1–2
 challenges Covey, 18
 childhood memories of, 54
 influence of Psalms on, 10
 motive for writing, 19
 Narrative as spiritual autobiography, 9
 on escaping, 12
 on origins of slavery, 61
 on significance of freedom, 61–62
 significance of *Narrative*, 3–4
 thoughts of future by, 2
DuBois, W. E. B., on slave autobiographies, 15
Dumas, Alexandre, 122

Eli (slave), 75, 113n. 44,
Ellison, Ralph, 15
Emancipation, Douglass's predictions of, 41
Employment
 Douglass on Blacks in skilled, 144
 of Douglass as ship caulker, 93
 wages of Douglass, 94, 95
Escape, 3
 by sea, 86–87
 details of Douglass's successful, 114n. 60

Douglass plans for first attempt at, 85–86
Douglass plans for second attempt at, 97
Douglass's constant thoughts on, 11–12
Douglass's conversation about, 62–63
Douglass's explanation for not divulging details of, 94
failure, 88–89
success, 98
Ewery, Rev., 69

Family separation, theme of, 13
Fairbanks, Wright, 69, 84
Farms, Lloyd's, 43
Father, Douglass on his, 40
Feminist critics, 18
Fights
 with Covey, 78, 79
 with white apprentices, 91
Food, 44, 54
Free Blacks
 as shipbuilding carpenters, 91
 spirit of Northern, 103
Freedom
 Douglass's quest for, 85
 fear of capture in, 86
 liquor as substitute for, 81
 obstacles to, 85
Freeland, Betsy, 89
Freeland, William, 81
 assessment of, 84–85
 character of, 81–82
 compared to Covey, 83
 rehires Douglass, 85
Friendship, 85, 98
Fugitive slaves, 99, 129
Fuller, Margaret
 biographical information, 121–122
 on Douglass, 16–17
 on Douglass as speaker, 122
 on Garrison introduction, 123
 on Phillips introduction, 123
 on religion and slavery, 123
 "Review of *Narrative* . . .," 121–123

Gardner, William
 as shipbuilder for slave trade, 114n. 57
 Douglass works in shipyard of, 91
 lynch law in shipyard of, 92